One Nature Indivisible

Explorations in Freethought

Chris Highland

CHRIS HIGHLAND

© 2022 Chris Highland

Friendly Freethinker (www.chighland.com)

All photographs by the author

Other Books by Chris Highland

From Faith to Freethought
Simply Secular
Nature is Enough
Friendly Freethinker
Broken Bridges
A Freethinker's Gospel
Birds, Beetles, Bears and Beliefs
Was Jesus a Humanist?
A Secular Gospel
Once Upon a Faith
Beyond the Boundaries of Belief
Highland Views
Intersections
The Message on the Mountain
Breath, Death and Koheleth
Meditations of John Muir (in a six-book series)
My Address is a River
Jesus and John Muir (novella)

"PERSPECTIVES"

I wrote this upside-down poem after reading "Pretty Ugly" attributed to Abdullah Shoaib. A theist reads from top to bottom, an a-theist reads from bottom to top

God is there
So please don't tell me
There's nothing greater than Nature
I don't see why someone can't see
The universe is a wondrous mystery
Others think science and reason are the way
While believers say "believe, trust and pray"
Faith points above, behind, beyond
While there's suffering, darkness, despair and death
I seek for wisdom, what is true and right and good
I wonder at the incredible Beauty of it all
The rivers and forests and oceans
The smallest creatures, the highest mountains
The stars and suns, planets and moons
Because when I consider this amazing world
How could I say there is no Creator?

{Now read bottom up}

Chris Highland
2021

CONTENTS

Introduction
1-Secrets of the Universe
2-What Have You Really Seen Today?
3-Ubuntu: A Secular Response to Spiritual Questions
4-The Greatest Love of All
5-Is There a "Natural Spirituality"?
6-Ego de Lego (You Have Heard that it was Said)
7-What Ever Happened to the Golden Rule?
8-Frames of Faith & Points of Reference
9-Religious Morality & Secular Ethics
10-Disturbing Disruptions/Insightful Interruptions
11-Paul Dunbar & the Heart of Happy Hollow
12-The Devil's in the Details: Do We Still Need Satan?
13-If We Applied Our Minds to Know Wisdom
14-Do Different Paths Lead to the Same Peak?
15-The Thinking Earth & the Laughing Tree
16-Three Mothers
17-The Sticky Note God
18-The Sweetness of Light in the Blink of an Eye
19-The Elimination of the Unthinkable
20-The Coffin Confessor
21-Olaudah Equiano: Slave, Sailor, Scribe
22-Preachers in Public Schools
23-Cherry-Picking & Tomato-Throwing
24-Seneca, Wisdom & Living Well with Nature
25-If Everyone Believed the Same as I Do

26-Sagan Saves Us from the Demon-Haunted World
27-Does Rising from the Dead Matter?
28-When Flora & Fauna are "Friends"
29-1619 and Beyond
30-Build a Bridge, then Get Over It
31-From the Moon to Making Meaning
32-The Benefit of a Basement Perspective
33-Henry Thoreau's Woodsy Meditations
34-The Nones Bible: Chapter One
35-The Nones Bible: Chapter Two
36-The Nones Bible: Chapter Three
37-The Nones Bible: Chapter Four
38-The Nones Bible: Chapter Five
39-The Nones Bible: Chapter Six
40-The Nones Bible: Chapter Seven
41-When Things Don't Add Up
42-Primitive, Childlike, Yet the Most Precious Thing
43-First Question: What's Really Going On?
44-Is a Creator Playing Hide-and-Seek?
45-Opening Thoughts at the Closing of the Book(s)
About the Author

INTRODUCTION

> *"Most people are on the world, not in it—have no conscious sympathy or relationship to anything about them...touching, but separate."*
> ~John Muir, Journal, July 1890

Freethinking isn't all that different from hiking, walking or sauntering, even in one's neighborhood or yard. Except it's a never-ending trek into ideas and most often the environment is unfamiliar. Freethinkers thrive on the exercise, the fresh air of fresh thoughts gained from the effort of getting up off the seat of our perspectives, picking up a question-mark-shaped walkingstick, and risking the adventure. This is all to say it's in our nature to explore Nature, and the nature of our own minds. Open trails for the feet, and the brain. We can't get far without what's in our boots or under our hat.

Those of us in the United States are used to "The Pledge." Even when we no longer participate and don't think the rote ritual is necessary to prove patriotism, we have it imprinted on our minds. In the 1950's, during the Eisenhower administration and the "Red Scare," the phrase "One nation indivisible" was magically (Congressionally) altered to "One nation *under God*, indivisible," and of course that small addition is anything but small. In the name of unity they added one of the most disunifying, divisive words. Is there a God and if so, which one? And why transform a statement of national allegiance into a statement of allegiance to faith? The Constitution is clear there should be "no religious test" for public office, yet it seems belief in a god, any god, is an unspoken requirement for respect and representation in modern America. Now, it's a spoken, expected requirement. In our divided time, even a promise to be loyal to unity rings empty.

Interjection: Is this our *Red Scare* moment that's actually a *Blue Scare*--fear of "Lib-socialists" and their progressive principles? Maybe the fear we hear exposes the old terror of the non-White, an irrational kind of *White Scare*. White supremacist nationalism. The fear-flag flies over the land: Red, White and Blue. Just a thought.

As John Muir might say, let's put this bluster and

blunder aside and return to the crucial center: Nature is *indivisible*. It is one whole thing made of all things. Step back for a moment (which we really can't from nature, but give it a try) and consider the flip side: Nature is *infinitely divisible*, always and forever divisible into infinite parts, an incomprehensible collection of everything. Ceaseless evolution and devolution, creation and destruction, birth and death, construction and deconstruction … and so on for eternity. Amen, so be it?

Where does this realization, this awareness, lead us? Back to the basics of our own humanity and how we "fit in" to the natural order/disorder. I would suggest what we're left with is to pledge allegiance to Nature. Here's what I mean by that odd statement.

A number of years ago, when I strummed my guitar more regularly, I wrote a simple, perhaps simplistic song called "The Matriot's Anthem," a kind of hymn to Mother Earth. I grew uncomfortable with patriotic songs and rituals that honor or even reverence one nation over all others. The Fatherland way of thinking seems foreign to me—pun intended. I have always honored the land of my birth, the country I call home, yet in some sense I suppose I outgrew the belief that America, one patch of the earth, was home when the whole planet is the actual habitation—especially given our internet and nuclear age I have no doubt that broader, borderless viewpoint was initially ignited by a more inclusive sense of what I used to call spirituality.

I had already begun to outgrow my Christian faith, branching into diverse landscapes of religious experience, working as an interfaith chaplain seeking to lower the defenses and defensiveness at the walls that separate and divide fellow inhabitants of the "home-planet." As "Matriot's Anthem" expressed this musically (to the tune of "America the Beautiful":

"Oh beautiful diversity, third planet from the sun, a spinning ball of land and sea, embracing every one ... Oh Planet Earth, Oh Planet Earth, our only Motherland, in every tongue, of every race, no borders, hand in hand. Of mountains wrapped in glistening snow, and river waterfalls, of trees to climb and paths to find, our song will break all walls. Now listen for the cry of hope, that opens every soul, and work to make the Good and Just, a bell of freedom toll."

Perhaps not the most creative lines, but the message still rings true, at least for me.

The photographs in this book are images of this concept of indivisibility. Bubbles, spiders, flowers, branches--all living symbols of the diversified unity, the many parts and the wholeness as well. A kind of matriotism perhaps we need now more than ever.

We are one nation under nature, one species under nature, one part, one very small part. Even saying "under" is misleading. As the biblical writer Koheleth (Ecclesiastes) asked: "Is there anything new under the sun?" (and of course there is). We are not "under" the sun, we are traveling around it. We are one world spinning around a celestial fireball (or one tribe sitting around an immense firepit). That image is not easy to warm up to, but I find that rather humbling, don't you? If we were "under God" I truly don't know what that means. Under divine rule and authority? Well, that still doesn't tell us much. Merely applying chosen texts from ancient papyrus to our contemporary lives makes little sense, so let's just say we aren't actually "under" anyone, on earth or in the heavens. We are *in* nature, integral, embedded, not subservient to it. We need laws and ethical guidance, but those are intrinsic to who we are as rational human beings. We are not "under" them.

I'm obviously no naturalist and definitely not a scientist, but I am a thinkist, aware of how challenging it is to think sometimes, to reason through my thoughts to some kind of conclusions, however tentative. Honestly I have to admit I don't fully trust myself to say I "know" something. But as Wendell Berry lays it out: "The first responsibility of intelligence [is] to know when you don't know or when you are being unintelligent." This honesty counteracts the "arrogant ignorance" that we see so much in our day ("The Way of Ignorance").

So here you have, in your hands, some of my thoughts to run them through your thoughts and see if anything holds true for you. Seriously, I have a very simple intent with my essays, columns and blogposts: to place my thoughts and questions before a reader to see what another person thinks. I have no hidden agenda or ulterior motive to convince anyone how right I am. No need to follow along the trail I choose.

If anything is intrinsically good, Nature is good. Destructive? Yes. Source of disease and death? Of course. Yet endlessly creative, surprising, mysterious, wonderful. There's always something new "under the sun." I would pledge my allegiance to Nature if necessary. Yet, grateful to Goodness, it isn't.

Chris Highland, 2022

For Rob
and
Deerhaven

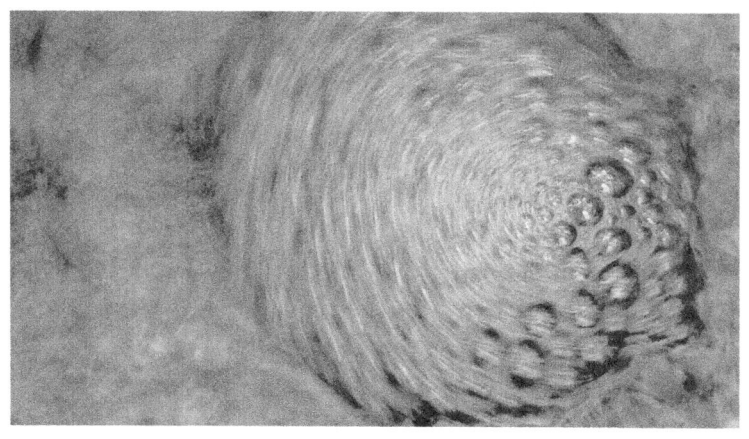

1
Secrets of the Universe

Never Before Seen by Human Eyes

The thought comes to me more frequently these days, regularly, consistently: *We are great in our smallness.* Humans are hugely important—in our own minds. We are the center of the universe—we imagine. All the world's religions say that a god, goddess or gods occupy eons of divine time with special concern for their special, masterpiece creation: Humanity. Divinities not only live for, but some gods are willing to die for, these little specks of dust, blood and bone. Aren't we something.

Then Science comes along and ruins our self-image! No wonder so many are anti-Science. It just won't tell us what we want to know. As Carl Sagan wrote: "If we long to believe that the stars rise and set for us, that we are the reason there is a Universe, does science do us a disservice in deflating our conceits?" (*The Demon-Haunted World*). Yet, we know; if we really think the hard thoughts, the uncomfortable thoughts, we know: We aren't that special. Among mammals, all living things, all the stars and planets, galaxies and whatever else is out there ... we are infinitesimally tiny, and sorry to say, insignificant—except to ourselves, and the religions we create, and the Big Ego Gods we make to boost our egos.

Here's what boosted my interest in recent days. Dang if it's not NASA again. Not the NASA that cozies up to politicians, generals and billionaires in their obsession with "using the resources" of the moon and mars, but the NASA consisting of scientists who are the daily explorers, those going where no one has gone before ... and will probably never go. Tiny people thinking big, really big. In fact, they are gazing out into stuff we can't even comprehend. Sound like religion? Maybe similar.

"Some 4.4 million space objects billions of light-years away have been mapped by astronomers, including 1 million space objects that hadn't been spotted before." This astounding discovery was reported on CNN's "Space and Science" page (February 25, 2022).

The survey "logged the radio signals of almost 300,000 galaxies and other space objects ... Each time we create a map our screens are filled with new discoveries and objects that have never before been seen by human eyes." This has our indivisible attention.

"We anticipate it will lead to many more scientific breakthroughs in the future, including examining how the largest structures in the universe grow, how black holes form and evolve, the physics governing the formation of stars in distant galaxies and even detailing the most spectacular phases in the life of stars in our own Galaxy," so says one scientist.

It took the computing power of 20,000 laptops! A massive amount of juice just to peer into the dark corners of the cosmos—though it's clear there are no corners and it's not all dark.

Who else claims to show us the "secrets of the universe"? We are told there are "far-seeing" teachers who gaze into the inner galaxies. Where do they get the super-natural ability to see or think or hear beyond our own range of senses? How much computer power, or brain power, are they utilizing? Do we trust them? How, and why? So many questions to probe, so many skeptical satellites to send into orbit.

And what of the unseen nearer at hand? For instance, the bacteria on our hands, on our bodies. The cells, atoms and molecules that make the incredible complexity of every human body. Isn't the human being, body and mind, a world, even a universe, still unmapped, unexplored? What secrets are still to be discovered within ourselves? Think if we didn't have the shiny attractions and heavenly distractions of other worlds and bodies. Understanding ourselves could use billions of brains and millions of laptops. What a universe at our fingertips!

How tuned is your telescope? Are the lenses clean and clear? Where do you aim it? What do you see? What do you *not* see but imagine is out there? And don't forget a microscope for the quest.

2
What Have You Really Seen Today?

A neighbor sends a note. He and his wife spotted a Cooper's hawk soaring over the wild field across the way. On an afternoon walk we stop by a shallow, still pond to check on tiny black tadpoles slowly growing in their bubble-clump attached to a small twig. We gently lift a tiny baby turtle off the road. Rustling leaves in a tree alert us to a startled bear cub sliding down.

Today, while pausing in my tappings on the keyboard, our chipmunks ran by, jowls jammed with nuts and seeds. A squirrel scurries by with a large pod in its chops; a rabbit bounds across the lawn. A crow woke me up early before the squawking led to the dawn chorus of wrens, jays, towhees, cardinals, doves, titmice, chickadees and finches. Who directs this choir of the morning? Who conducts this symphony of sound?

As I see it, and hear it, a concerted effort is required to fully appreciate the gift of the wild nearby. And I think that appreciative curiosity is directly related to health, especially mental health. The immersive sensate experience of wildness at hand may also correspond to any meaningful sense of religious sensitivity or awareness.

I admit, it may be easier for me to see these wild things since I live in the wild biodiversity of the Blue Ridge Mountains. One niece who studies at Appalachian State told me her most interesting class is Biology; her excitement was evident as she told us she is learning how wide a diversity of species thrives in these mountains. Her boyfriend is majoring in Biological Sciences and wants to train as an anesthesiologist. I found it very encouraging to see these young people drawn to the essential lessons of life and living. They enjoyed seeing my photographs of an orange newt, millipede, cicada and katydid. My niece wasn't so thrilled to see my closeup of a jumping spider. Hopefully her fears will diminish as she studies more of the ecological balance that is Life on Earth.

It is no doubt more challenging if you live in a city, a more urban environment. You may not have the time to observe all the life around when working or focused on finding work or food or shelter. If you have a lot of pressures and there are many things to do, to get done, you can't be troubled to stop and listen, to learn what's near. Yet, I would hope you will be troubled to do it! It's worth the trouble, and it won't be troubling, to take a few minutes to see something new, to hear something different, to feel something that might give a new thought to enliven your day, your life.

Yet, this is something to consider. Being "troubled" by the stresses of life. So many distractions, attractions to grab and nab our attention. The business at hand may be all we have energy for, though a fresh recharge may be available, and necessary.

My question, for you and for myself, is: why do the wisest teachers call attention to plants and animals, using images and crafting parables from the natural environment? Why does the Bible begin with a garden and end by a river and tree?

A popular tune we sang with jail inmates and homeseekers was "Look all around you and see what is real, hear what is true and be sure what you feel." This applies to the wildness of the human community as it does to the wilderness around us. It can be as simple as looking around, hearing, feeling … and responding with a sense of responsibility.

In my description of the parade of wildlife across their land (yes, theirs) I neglected to mention the insects and the species of creaturely neighbors I can't identify. It's become a principle practice for me to spy living things I've never seen and stay aware and attentive to the very real possibility that *no one has ever seen what I'm seeing* from day to day. Even if a biologist or naturalist has seen, recorded, named a critter, it's still a unique and delightful new discovery for me.

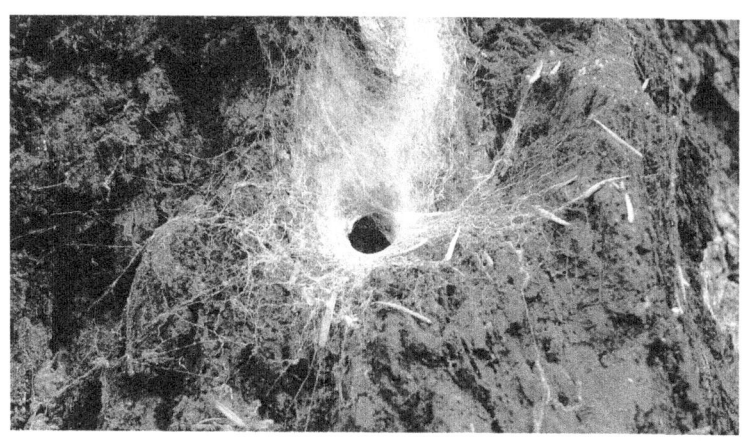

3
Ubuntu: A Secular Response to Spiritual Questions

I first encountered Ubuntu as a font, one among the hundreds of designs for letters. Artists create lines and loops for letters so we can be expressive with the words and sentences we form, when our "words become flesh"—or ink. A particular font may enhance our ability to communicate something more than a mere word on a page; it potentially adds a flair or flourish to what it is we want to communicate. We might also say that a word in Ubuntu font can draw the eye to something behind the letter, beneath the word, even beyond the original intent of the writer.

In the world's scriptures, font matters, that is, the

presentation makes a difference. Arabic passages from the Qur'an are creatively drawn, artwork in themselves. When English speakers see Hebrew or Sanskrit, Pali or Greek, there is a curiosity to interpret not only the words but the person behind the words, the writer-artist who crafted the text. This may be more interesting than the "holy words" themselves.

Consider the meaning of the word "Ubuntu" itself. The human person behind the word Ubuntu can show us how it can be packed to the font with meaning. Viewing a short video on BBC REEL, "The Philosophy that can change how you look at life," I was struck by an African professor's explanation of the concept of "Ubuntu," an indigenous philosophy that translates: "I am because you are" (or, "I am because of who we all are"). As professor James Ogude of the University of Pretoria, South Africa, explains, it's about "interdependence, we rely on each other." It's not political or religious but, "a social awareness, a consciousness of the fact we all have a responsibility to ourselves as human beings, especially the vulnerable among us ... and a responsibility to the world around us." He uses the example of bees that pollinate so much of our food crops. Caring for them is intimately connected to caring for ourselves. We are reminded of "co-agency"—working together with all life to nurture Life.

Professor Ogude makes a distinction between "individuality" and "individualism." Individuality offers a sense of independence and freedom.

Individualism is about "me, me, me, all the time ... the ego." Living in community reminds us we are inter-responsible as our individuality is dependent on the community.

Not wanting to sound like an Ubuntu missionary, he wants to direct our attention to the great value of indigenous knowledge around the world. He believes that if we want to imagine a healthy society in the future, concepts from the past, like Ubuntu, can guide our thinking and our working. The sense of mutuality is critical. Here he points to Archbishop Desmond Tutu who led his country in challenging apartheid, drawing from past values to forever change South Africa.

One of professor Ogude's most practical examples is greeting another, really acknowledging their presence and value. Even ordering a meal or drink, "recognition is fundamental." Speaking a person's name, showing respect for their identity, their unique individuality.

He concludes with a story a friend told him about fishermen in the Amazon. When they catch a lot of fish, they throw some back, honoring the fact the river sustains them, it feeds them, "it's a source of life." To summarize the concept of Ubuntu, professor Ogude, with little hesitation, responds: "interdependence."

Ubuntu seems a more humanistic as well as naturalistic response to traditional spiritual questions. In the African Journal of Social Work

(August 2013) this preliminary definition appears: "Ubuntu echoes the African thought of acceptable ideas and deeds. Ubuntu can best be described as humanism from the African perspective." In Africa, Ubuntu has been applied in theology, politics, management and computer science. The essence of the practice is: "To affirm one's humanity by recognizing the humanity of others."

We might think of it in these ways:

-What is the meaning or purpose of life? Ubuntu responds: to learn how we are interdependent; meaning comes through the way we treat others.
-Is there a God? Ubuntu responds: There may be. But this doesn't change the first response.
-When we look for guidance and values from the past, shouldn't we look to scriptures before anything else? Ubuntu responds: Wherever we find the wisdom that guides us to practice respectful compassion toward others and toward the earth, it is good.
-What about rituals of prayer and worship? Ubuntu responds: Again, if these actions encourage a mutuality and responsibility toward others, it is good.
-What happens to religious belief and faith? Ubuntu responds: Beliefs are fine, as long as the essential belief is that "I am because you are."

With an awareness of cultural appropriation, Ubuntu seems to be a "font of wisdom" for all cultures.

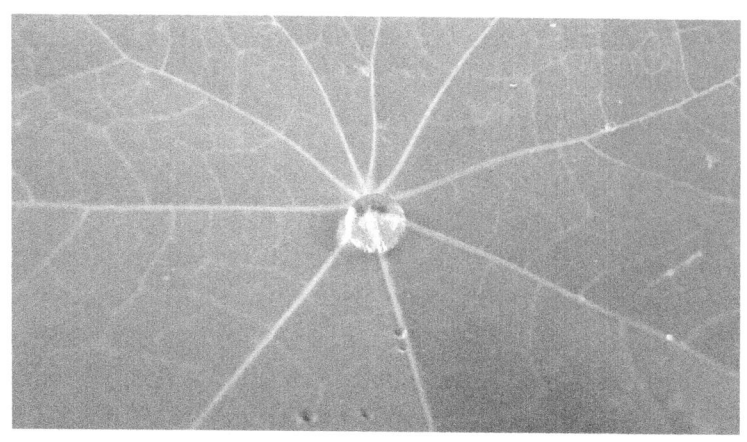

4
Looking for Lessons for Living the Greatest Love of All

Think test: "No one has greater love than this ..." Can you finish the sentence? "Than to have faith"? "Than to be more religious"? No. "No one has greater love than this, to lay down one's life for one's friends" (John 15:13). Jesus of Nazareth said a lot about love. Bible students and preachers make much of different Greek words for love—friendly love, godly love, etc—yet, doesn't it all come back to practicing something that matters, that makes a difference in people's lives? I'm guessing Jesus was after a quality of life regardless of semantic squabbles over what the word love means. Does "greater" mean an amount of love, a quantity, or a quality? Who are we willing to lay down our lives for? Only for "friends"? Did Jesus live, teach and die only for his "friends"? I don't think that's the traditional Christian story.

While driving to college classes in 1970's Seattle, I often played a tape of George Benson singing the song, "The Greatest Love of All." The lyrics were written by Linda Creed for the 1977 film, "The Greatest," about Muhammad Ali. The song is a kind of anthem for self-reliance, with a genuine concern for the self-determination of the next generation.

"I believe the children are our future, teach them well and let them lead the way; show them all the beauty they possess inside; give them a sense of pride, to make it easier; let the children's laughter remind us how we used to be." This inspiring verse follows: "Everybody's searching for a hero, someone to look up to, I never found anyone to fulfill my needs; a lonely place to be, so I learned to depend on me." There's a powerful sense of self-confidence in the words: "I decided long ago, Never to walk in anyone's shadow; if I fail, if I succeed, at least I'll live as I believe; no matter what they take from me, they can't take away my dignity." Finally, the chorus: "Because the greatest love of all, is happening to me, I found the greatest love of all inside of me." (I recommend Whitney Houston's rendition on YouTube).

The song encourages looking inward: "The greatest love of all is easy to achieve, learning to love yourself, is the greatest love of all." Does this correlate with

Jesus' teaching to give one's life for someone familiar? The song says it begins with inner acceptance, believing in our own gifts. It has been said, "God is love," but what if you don't believe in God? In matters of lovingkindness, does it matter? If a person lives by love and says that's divine while another person practices a loving life and says that's simply "in my nature," the result is the same. Love cannot be forced or commanded, though we hear the Nazarene Teacher say: "This is my commandment, that you love one another as I have loved you." To truly love your neighbor as yourself (a teaching from the book of Leviticus) you have to choose to draw from the deep well within, to have the dignity, the courageous core of inner strength that the song calls for, to love yourself first. Then ... to encourage others to love themselves too. That may be one of the greatest gifts we can pass along to another, especially the young.

Linda Creed, who wrote the lyrics to "The Greatest Love of All," collaborated to write some other hits including songs for the Stylistics and the Spinners ("You Make Me Feel Brand New," "Ghetto Child," "The Rubber Band Man"). Her personal story is no happy melody. According to Wikipedia: "Though diagnosed with breast cancer at 26, Creed kept on working, teaming with composer Michael Masser and writing the lyrics to the song "The Greatest Love of All" ... The lyrics of the song were written in the midst of her struggle with breast cancer. The words describe her feelings about coping with great challenges ...

whether you succeed or fail, and passing that strength on to children to carry with them into their adult lives … Creed died of breast cancer on April 10, 1986, at the age of 37."

In 1973, Linda Creed wrote, "Life is a Song Worth Singing" recorded by Johnny Mathis. Even then, her courage was clear as she could inspire with her great talent:

"Life is a song worth singing, Why don't you sing it? You hold the key in the palm of your hand, use it; Don't blame your life on the master plan, change it; Only you generate the power, to decide what to do with your life." This songwriter left us a soulful way to love who we are and sing it for others.

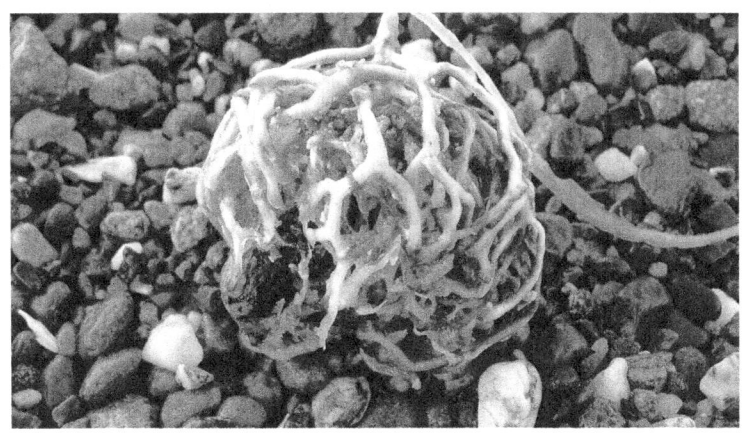

5
Is There a "Natural Spirituality"?

A book was published in 2010 entitled, *Life After Faith: Radical Paths to a Reasonable Spirituality*. The person who wrote that was Chris Highland and I beg to differ with his definitions and descriptions from over a decade ago.

The book was primarily written while I was living in a one-room cabin on Whidbey Island in my native Washington State. Other than clearing new trails in the dense forests surrounding my cabin (my first cabin was on 45 acres), I would spend hours sitting in my woodsy "office" typing on a laptop, until it rained or snowed or the wind blew down branches.

In one section of *Life After Faith*, I laid out what I

termed, "essentials of a natural spirituality." Again, the language I chose would not be the same today:

"A short running definition of "Natural Spirituality" is called for. Natural spirituality is being enrolled as a full-time student in the University of the Universe, learning the lessons Nature has to teach, participating in the liveliness of direct experience and growing a pragmatic livelihood from the roots up. Practicing a natural spirituality has everything to do with nurturing a participatory relation to Nature and Spirit (another honorific name for Nature) in a practice that integrates lessons from the natural world of which one is a part in order to see and experience a wider wisdom while working for the greater integration and inter-relation of the greater good."

Continuing this path of reasoning I drew an example from my "Pathfinder" trail work. I was sweating and straining one day in the warm spring sun, pulling up blackberry vines by the roots. While I was aware of the harm (and often apologized even to the bladed whips scratching me head to foot) I pulled out a lesson or two drenched in blood and sweat. This was my "participation in the liveliness of direct experience" with Nature as I could "see and experience a wider wisdom" while working with the land where I live. My natural spirituality was literally "at work" digging down in those roots with my mattock. The deep holding on of the network of tendrils was impressive, and fully exhausting.

The loop of a trail I opened through the forest was a related project for the day and reminded me that wherever we live we displace some living things, and sometimes this displacement appears to open up new relationships with the land and the community of living things. When I am in this close contact, covered in earth and leaves and sticks, lifting slugs, beetles, treefrogs and worms out of harm's way, I see what I have never seen before and though I am always aware of the disruption I am causing, I am even more encouraged with the thought that my work will bring me, and I will bring others, closer to this earth, this land. My labors are my way of introducing one species to another. This is especially true with people who have never seen large parts of their own land (not that every square inch must be revealed to human eyes). To me this means they are never fully rooted themselves. Their appreciation is clear in their exclamations of wonder and sometimes in their tears of enjoyment and silent awe."

With these images in mind I continued forward, moving as I thought "down the twisted trails to an appreciation of what is at the heart of natural spirituality. Here are some "roots" (arteries) that I have identified for any participant in relation to the earth—living vines of wisdom for those of us who are delighted and startled by life.

One: A deep respect, interest and feeling for Nature as matrix for one's life and a Teacher and Guide;

the growing, greening world, earth, planet, worldwide ecosystems, universal context; a love of the wilderness near and far and commitment to preserve the living, wild sources and resources.

Two: A deep respect, interest and feeling for Spirit (the non-supernatural "Presence" of Nature; an honorific title) as the interconnecting whole encircling and interweaving all things on the planet and beyond; the vision of the "higher purposes" or "deeper meanings" that set life in motion and call to stillness. A sinking in.

Three: A recognition that Nature, the natural world that includes the nature of the human person, is the first and primary "Text" for reading and mapping out the way, for seeking guidance and for sacred knowledge. At least a basic familiarity with the sacred texts of the world's wisdom traditions (the Old Maps from which to draw the new outlines for encompassing navigation). A plan to learn more.

Four: An understanding that Nature is chapel, church, temple, mosque and synagogue, and yet is more; that the spiritual life transcends any particular structure, belief system, geographic limitation, intellectual bias or community; it is organic and sustainable; it is a grounded, and grounding, grove, meadow or mountaintop in constant stillness, consistent motion.

Five: A working knowledge of the fundamental teachings of the major wisdom/religion/spiritual traditions (the Old World from which to embark on voyages of discovery). A respect for those teachings that are respectable (those that can be, so to speak, downloaded and run without a virus). A plan to learn more.

Six: A delighted curiosity and questioning attitude in general (not necessarily a skepticism) and a desire to learn and grow in understanding of the world as it is and as it could be. An explorer's heart, an inventor's mind.

Seven: A "Work" that provides the central environment for an active, practical and natural spirituality. Seeking to integrate one's work (to earn money for living) with one's Work (to act consciously with the meaning of living). An openness to new ways of livelihood. A commitment to research and be involved in current projects touching natural spirituality, inter-working with local, regional, national and global projects as needed.

Eight: A philosophy and practice of caretaking and caregiving as these relate directly and vitally with the natural, secular world particularly in the causes of environmental justice and human rights.

As I understood it all then, these eight principles shape "the essence of natural spirituality, at least in my mind. They are much more organic and sustainable than those commands hammered into stone. These guiding notes to carry in our mental pockets as we sit or walk deeper in the natural world will grow and expand with each fresh and nurturing participant who grows in conscious appreciation of the practice."

In the Appendices, I attempted more description through a summary: "Natural Spirituality: What it is, and isn't."

"There are many potential responses to the modern religious community and its non-monolithic yet lithographic agenda. In this book I offer one viable, organic alternative: *Natural Spirituality*. It holds the most pragmatic promise and hope to counter the suicidal sinking of religion."

This led to a section I called "Many Rivers":

Natural spirituality is freethinking at its best: free-flowing and unafraid to change, adapt, grow, think, learn and stand for freedom in all spheres of our lives. It is a practice not unlike a river freely meandering through different territories, picking up pieces of living matter, pushing aside intransigent rocks and giving vital water to the land, regardless of the artificial borders, fences, bridges or barriers. Natural Spirituality is a river practice, equally "at home" in synagogue, church, mosque, temple, classroom, office, lab. . . but most "at home" in the Great Open Temple of Nature. For this reason a nature-based spirituality finds its scriptures and rituals in the expansive landscape open to all.

A river becomes not merely a metaphor but a teacher. All dissolves into basic elements as "river" becomes Water, Earth, currents of Air and lava flows of Fire, as well as wild, migratory movement on land, in the air, on the sea. A waterway, like a tree or any other lifeform, becomes not simply a venerated symbol but a living companion. The "river community" becomes a deepening, ever-surprising source of nourishment, wholeness, inclusion, living in relation with all creatures and all of creation.

Here are a few things that Natural Spirituality is and is not

*It IS a practice that has sustained integrity and balance based on reason as well as feeling. It welcomes and assumes all inquiry of science and philosophy.
It is NOT a new age mishmash of feel-good spirituality.
*It IS interested in drawing the best from all water sources, that is, all wisdom sources, including but not limited to the wise wells of the ages.
It is NOT interested in digging one central well or damming all the rivers of faith to channel them into one tamed, controlled "sacred" river.
*It IS concerned with bringing diverse people together to learn in common environments as we act responsively and responsibly together.
It is NOT yet another "dialogue group" where people simply compare creeds and rituals, merely study and talk or engage in political debate.
*It IS drawn to courageous thinking and courageous action that challenges and changes.
It is NOT supportive of religious communities that

rarely or never take a stand, or worse, take public positions that counter or threaten Nature or Reason.
*It IS motivated by the beauty of Nature and the best of humans in partnership with Nature.
It is NOT satisfied with fear-driven faith motivated by obeisance and otherworldly goals and concerns.

It is "the most ancient religion," to borrow a line from Emerson. It is prime, primary, the most primitive practice there is. It has always been. It is the most present awareness and activity, as well as the most relevant and constructive lifeway for the future. While it underlies the origins of all the historic religions as a subterranean stream, as a root or as a ground, it can never be fully held in any vessel, container-box, walled garden or holy land. It is not "native" to any one land or tribe but is indigenous wherever practiced. It is interested in discussing but not arguing theological perspectives and opinions because it is committed to exploring and analyzing all understandings of the divine, as long as such exploration does not distract from grounded work. Because of its openness ("it" is not open, those who practice it are open) and its willingness to learn from all wisdom, it also welcomes reasonable insight from those who hold to no particular theological belief. In fact, we are calling this a "spirituality" in recognition of the fluid, playful, usually specific but often nebulous nature of an open practice of the sacred (another problematic term). It could just as easily be understood as Path or Way (in a Taoist sense for instance) or simply: the balanced, interrelated Life.

The mystic rabbi, Abraham Joshua Heschel, once wrote, "Religion becomes sinful when it begins to advocate the segregation of God, to forget that the true sanctuary has no walls"(*God in Search of Man*).

If rabbi Heschel is correct, that religion is destructive when it says God is apart or distant, that religion is evil when it does not see and participate with the world as divine, that religion is wrong when it sets apart sacrosanct sanctuaries with literal and creedal walls, fencing its God inside and excluding all that makes up the wide-open and true holy place of the universe. . .if rabbi Heschel is right, what are we left with? Everywhere we look, religion is sinful, destructive, dangerous—at the very least unhelpful and unhealthy. Only a heretic can say these things with force and determination—a heretical mystic like Moses, Buddha, Jesus, Mohammad, Hildegard, Rumi, Mirabai, Muir, Burroughs and ordinary mystics who are intimately related to the "gospel of the present moment."

My conclusions, debated in my mind to this day, seriously call into question all the language I've used. It seems clear I was trying hard to hold-the-old, the language of past worldviews, and breathe new life into them, even as they crumbled in my hands.

"The naturally spiritual way or path is not so concerned with tearing down but building up. We see no need to eliminate all the churches and other sanctuaries from the earth. No need to burn all the scriptures and put all the clergy out of work. Not yet! Not until we re-imagine and re-create a spiritual practice that fully honors the earth, our own earthiness and the "divinity" or "miracle" in every particle, spark and quark; a spiritual practice that does not advocate a segregation of divinity/spirit walled out of all our experience but advocates an integration of the sacred (unifying) ideals into every aspect of life on earth. This is a spiritual practice of honesty, openness, health, reason, responsibility, creativity and hope. This is the way ahead, a spiritual practice that can only be called Natural."

Now, I would simply rephrase this: The way ahead is a path of wisdom that is fundamentally Natural. Any "spiritual" words are obstacles and distractions on the trail; they are unhelpful and no longer necessary, naturally.

6
You Have Heard it Said, *Ego de Lego*

There are teachers and there are preachers. Those who have thoughtful lessons to convey not only pass along knowledge but helpful ways to handle knowledge. In other words, teachers may use images and illustrations, field trips and guest speakers, many different modes of making knowledge interesting and practical. Those who preach, in the classic sense, are proclaiming, attempting to convince and perhaps convert listeners to beliefs or a set of doctrines to affirm and accept on the authority of the preacher.

Preachers have followers, teachers have students. Teachers and preachers present required reading to explore knowledge from past and present thinkers.

Preachers, at least in some religions, traditionally offer one primary book. They preach from that book with the expectation the words that are heard will be accepted as divinely inspired. Thus, the preaching is "expounding the Word of God" or "proclaiming the Gospel" with the intent to foster belief in the authority of God, the Word and the Preacher. Teachers, on the other hand, may also utilize ancient writings yet the intent is to ignite energetic engagement with the texts, and with everything the teacher teaches, to develop skeptical minds that question and search for rational answers; a good, competent educator "teaches students to teach themselves." At least we would expect that's the goal, though it may be unspoken or unconscious.

I'm obviously oversimplifying and I acknowledge there are teachers who also preach and preachers who also teach. Yet I think it's wise to consider the intentions, what the speaker expects from their class, audience or congregation. We still hear preachers who say or imply "God told me to tell you this" or "Here's what God thinks or feels about that." And, we sometimes hear of teachers who get preachy about their own biases. When that's admitted, it might be alright, but sometimes students may not be ready or able to discern if they are being asked to accept what the teacher knows as the "whole story." Fundamentally, a critical question is: How do we know?

Here's where I'm going with this. During a retreat

at a Buddhist center, I began reading a collection of scripture entitled "Thus Have I Heard." These are the teachings, sayings and stories of Gautama Buddha from the original text of the Pali canon. Passed down for thousands of years, the intent is to invite us to hear what they heard in ancient days. From the Teacher to the student-disciples, to villagers throughout Asia and beyond, down through the centuries. Once we've heard, we encourage others to hear, and so the listening link to the past connects to the present and on into the future. This is the "hearsay" that generates traditions in all cultures and religions. "Say, Hear!" is often the demand of hearsay, those who want us to accept or believe something just because they heard it, and believed it, themselves.

In his lecture on a Judean mountainside—sometimes called The Sermon on the Mount—the Teacher of Nazareth addressed some of the most enduring and endemic concerns for the human community (see Matthew 5-7). Though it may be hard to dig under centuries of supernaturalizing and sermonizing these teachings, I think it is still possible for our inter-religious and secular world to draw up some ethical guidance and wisdom from the well of time.

I suggest we learn this one phrase from the Greek language: "Ego de lego humin." It means "But I say to you." Jesus spoke Aramaic, but in the Gospels, written in Greek, the Teacher of Nazareth uses this phrase a number of times in his outdoor lecture. It usually follows "It is written" or "You have heard it said." This one Greek phrase may be one of the most important teachings in history, certainly religious history.

It's a powerful style of teaching—a kind of freethinker's mantra. "You've heard that ... but hear this." A quite radical thing to say. In essence it makes an astonishing claim: "You have heard your [scriptures and religious preachers and teachers] say ..., but ego de lego." It is written ... but now here's something to think about. Notice this assumes his hearers know the ancient texts; the words were familiar—they had heard or read these things before. But now, they are hearing a new twist, a fresh interpretation they may never have considered. The Hebrew scriptures offer instructions regarding human relationships. This Teacher has a new lesson plan, not to throw out the old, but to restore its relevance, bring it into the present and make it personal, practical.

Of course, 2000 years later, we are in need of other voices, other teachers, who startle us with their own, "Ego de lego humin."

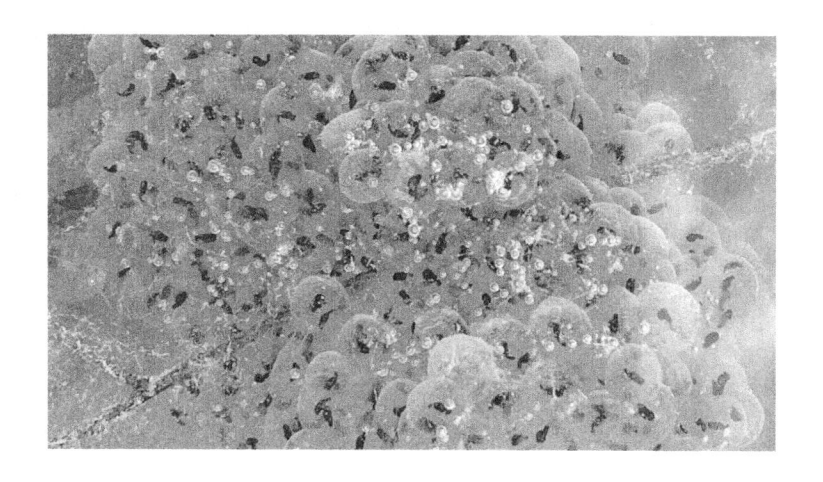

7
What Ever Happened to the Golden Rule?

For a class I was teaching on the Mountain Message (also known as the Sermon on the Mount), I kept stopping, stumbling, stuttering over Matthew chapter seven, verse twelve. We've all heard it, perhaps memorized it. With parallels in other faiths, it's known around the world, even quoted by people who aren't Christians. Slipped in near the end of the great outdoor lecture, the famous line appears: "All things that you wish other human beings would do for you (or to you), the same even you do for them (or to them)." Updating the phrase that follows this instruction we might say: "For this is all the scripture, all the religion, all the faith you need."

Read like this, what would happen to the Church, the Christian Religion and beliefs about Jesus and the Bible? As a teacher, I know how important it is to leave students with a few profound thoughts or ideas, something to reason with, to contemplate long after the class is over. A Philosophy professor in the Evangelical college I attended once wrote on the chalkboard: "The Power of an Idea." I've never forgotten that. I've carried that in the chalkdust of my memory ever since. Professor Johnson was a pious, conservative man, yet he also wrote on the chalkboard of our minds: "Conserve and Build." He thought conserving some things is a good idea—a powerful idea—and building upon a foundational idea was wise, like the GR, the Golden Rule.

Why call the famous principle "golden"? I suppose we do this because it's a precious treasure we value as a guide for life. It wasn't spoken by the Lecturer as a command so much as a guiding ethic, a rule of thumb as well as mind and heart (the Confucian principle of "reciprocity" is similar). The word "anthropos" is used in the Greek—"other human beings"—and I wonder if that's significant. Others are humans too, so do for them, or to them, just what you want for yourself.

Do we want to be respected, heard, included, treated justly and equally? Do we want to have enough to survive and thrive, to live safe and free, to be content? What is it we really want for ourselves? Once we've figured that out, as we're figuring that out, we ought to consider what others are figuring out for their lives. Do they want what we want? What if they want, or need, things we don't actually want, or need?

If this "rule" is ever to be "golden," a valuable and values-centered practice for life, it has to be taken seriously. The problem is that some who say they believe it don't seem to take it seriously. Take religion itself. Is a religious practice based on acting toward others in a thoughtful manner? To pressure others to believe as we do isn't treating them the way we wish to be treated. A secular practice of the GR should keep that in mind as well. I don't want to cause someone not to believe if that's their choice.

Now, I think there's something startling here, a powerful idea that builds on the conserving of everything that is good in us. The disturbingly wonderful questions is: What if the Teacher of Nazareth was, perhaps unconsciously, presenting the end of religion—at least the completion of religion as we've known it? Follow my reasoning here. He said this basic ethical principle was the Torah, the Bible. "For this IS the Law and the Prophets." Barring a whole bunch of theological gymnastics, we've stumbled onto the center of religion, the center of humanity itself—as we wish to be fully human, we wish that for others. End of story. The lesson: Do it; Live it. Religion, faith, theologies, bibles, can all be distractions drawing us away from the foundation—humanness, our own humanity.

Could it be the GR—potentially a central ethical principal of life—in and of itself, is the only religion we need, the only one that truly makes sense for the present and the future?

I find it intriguing that immediately prior to the mountain-climbing master's message, he is portrayed as a supernatural superstar healing everyone in sight. Then, immediately following his lecture, he descends from the mountain and the first thing he does is heal someone. We might wonder if the religion that made the super-human wonderworker the centerpiece of the whole story overshadowed many lessons from the Mountain Message, including perhaps the "heart" of the message itself.

It may be left to us, to those willing to climb these heights to hear this critical instruction, to reclaim the GR and our own humanity. This is the whole Torah, Gospel ... and Religion.

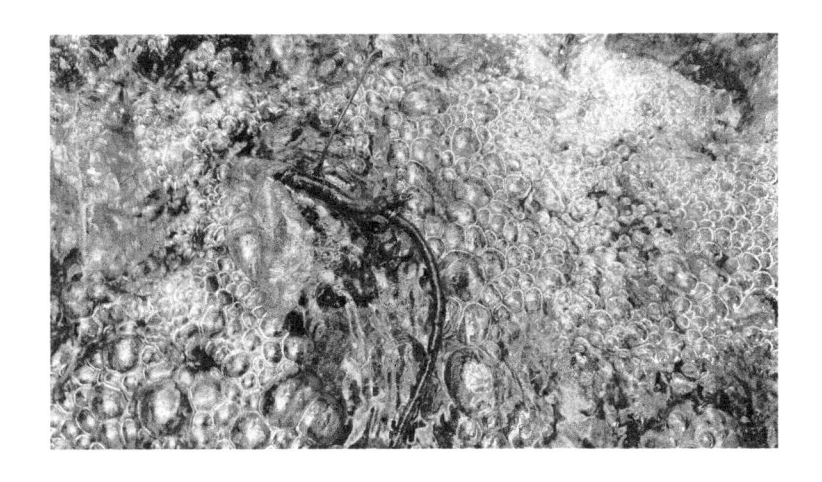

8
Frames of Faith & Points of Reference

Preparing to teach a class on books of the "old" and "new" testaments, I knew that one of the first lessons was to erase those words from our early Sunday School minds. There is no "old" testament, there is a Hebrew Bible. There in no "new" testament, there are Christian scriptures. In the Christian scriptures—Gospels, Letters of Paul, etc—we are told that early Christians believed they had a "new covenant," a fresh, new and improved agreement (testament), with the Almighty. Even a cursory scan of those early Christian texts makes clear there was a tension between the followers of the Jewish rabbi of Nazareth and the traditional Jewish community. Then, another fracturing controversy divided Jewish Christians and Gentile (non-Jewish)

Christians. You wouldn't have wanted to be in leadership during those disputes. Jesus was lucky to leave before that started.

This class preparation got me thinking about our frames of reference. How we see our world and then set standards in history marks not only where we came from but "where we're coming from" in our beliefs. Take for example the way the world dates history, particularly religious history. Most of us think we live in 2022, but what does that date mean? We are told it is 2022 A.D.—Anno Domini: in the year of our Lord. Of course this refers to the Christian Lord, Jesus, who was born around 2022 years ago (scholars debate the exact year). The time before that birth is called B.C.—Before Christ. For centuries the "Christian world" has been perfectly satisfied with a Gregorian calendar based on the birth of its divine child. But what of the rest of the world? Does everyone on the planet have to set their calendars and clocks to one religion's divine birth narrative?

In our day, many use a more inclusive, perhaps honest way of referring to the year: C.E.—Common Era (2022 in common understanding or agreement). And consider these other reference points in "sacred history":

—A.H.-Anno Hijri (1444 years since the Prophet Muhammad took flight, *hejira*, from Mecca to Medina in Arabia. C.E. 622)
—B.E.-Buddhist Era (2565 years since the time of

Gautama Buddha)
—Hebrew/Jewish Calendar (5782 years since the creation)

So, what year is it? A valid and valuable question given these variations across the globe. In my youthful missionary days we would often say that history was actually "His-Story"—all about Jesus beginning to end. Our church youth choir sang "One Solitary Life," based on a poem that essentially claimed Jesus stood at the center of world history (a Christian World, not merely a Christian Nation). The song we sang in choir proclaimed: "All the armies that ever marched, all the navies that ever set sail, all the rulers who ever ruled, all the kings that ever reigned on earth, have not effected the life of men on earth, like this One Solitary Life." Quite a claim. And there is no disputing the fact the life and teachings of Jesus of Nazareth have certainly shaped the course of much world history. But apart from those who are passionately devoted to that one individual, how can we ignore other significant individuals who set their own mark on the history of their people, and perhaps all of us? We don't live in a *Christian World*, we share a world where many people in many lands hold a wide spectrum of perspectives.

There obviously need to be some standards regarding dates, measurements, laws, ethics. But neither one person—a Caesar or Pope—nor one nation or religion can decree those. Diverse human beings may have very different cultural and religious histories. Who can dictate how to set universal standards? In the past it has indeed been "one solitary life," a powerful figure in one particular sectarian community who establishes what everyone must accept. Yet, how does that work in our world today, when there are so many frames of thought and points of reference?

This reminds me of the "trick" question: "Do they have a fourth of July in Canada?"

Pope Gregory, who commissioned his new calendar in 1582, was the one who appointed cardinals to draft the Index Librorum Prohibitorum ("Index of Forbidden Books"). He also established new seminaries to train missionaries to counter the Protestants in other countries. Eventually the new system of dating world history was accepted by all lands conquered and converted by powerful arms of Christendom (who controlled the official reading list). Anyone who asked: "What's the date today?" would be told: "It's this many years since *Our Lord* came to earth." Now we might reply: "But that's your point of reference. What about ours?"

9
Religious Morality & Secular Ethics

Consider this: "But for all its benefits in offering moral guidance and meaning in life, in today's secular world religion alone is no longer adequate as a basis for ethics." What immoral atheist wrote those words? The Dalai Lama of Tibet, 86-year-old spiritual leader for millions around the world. In his 2011 book, "Beyond Religion: Ethics for a Whole World," he explains that opening sentence: "One reason for this is that many people in the world no longer follow any particular religion. Another reason is that, as the peoples of the world become ever more closely interconnected in an age of globalization and in multicultural societies, ethics based in any one religion would only appeal to some of

53

us; it would not be meaningful for all."

I don't claim to remember much about Aristotle and his "Ethics" from my college Philosophy courses, but I do know he valued living well which leads to happiness and the good life. Living a good life is not simply a philosophical pursuit. For Aristotle, seeking the good isn't about gaining knowledge so much as a daily practice of well-being. He wrote: "[If] all people competed for the beautiful, and strained to do the most beautiful things, everything people need in common, and the greatest good for each in particular, would be achieved." As the Stanford Encyclopedia of Philosophy (SEP) states it: "If we use reason well, we live well as human beings; or, to be more precise, using reason well over the course of a full life is what happiness consists in …Doing anything well requires virtue or excellence …" There's a need for a wise balance. This gives us a lot to digest, but it's worth chewing on.

Those who set the high bars, establishing standards for what is good and bad, right and wrong, become our authorities for deciding those questions. Though they may not be good examples of the good and the right themselves, we consciously or unconsciously absorb their boundary lines. There are those who claim ancient books set the standards, that morality was set in stone (papyrus, vellum, paper) centuries ago. To be "religiously correct," we must abide by those guidelines, guardrails and rules. The biggest threat to these Morality Managers is the heretic, the freethinker, who questions, challenges and resists their authority. Name any founder of a religion and you've named a heretic. Just as abolitionist freethinker Lucretia Mott stood firm on her own standard of conscience: "Truth for authority, not authority for truth," so we may stand on "Good for authority, not authority for the Good." Without "God's Laws" and those who enforce them, how can we ground our lives in a meaningful goodness? Can personal happiness and fulfillment have an expansive and inclusive basis?

Returning to the Dalai Lama, he uses his own specific community as an example of our present dilemma: "In the past, when peoples lived in relative isolation from one another — as we Tibetans lived quite happily for many centuries behind our wall of mountains — the fact that groups pursued their own religiously based approaches to ethics posed no difficulties. Today, however, any religion-based answer to the problem of our neglect of inner values can never be universal, and so will be inadequate."

This honest self-reflection is essential to any forward progress. The wise teacher presents a solution to our propensity to get stuck in one worldview with its own concrete monument to morality. "What we need today is an approach to ethics which makes no recourse to religion and can be equally acceptable to those with faith and those without: a secular ethics." He understands this may be confusing, since he is a Buddhist monk. But he's concerned for the good lives of others beyond his own faith. He's confident that a sincere practice of a truly happy life will have wide impact. "My confidence comes from my conviction that all of us, all human beings, are basically inclined or disposed toward what we perceive to be good. Whatever we do, we do because we think it will be of some benefit. At the same time, we all appreciate the kindness of others. We are all, by nature, oriented toward the basic human values of love and compassion."

Aristotle, as I'm reminded, reflected on the idea "when the good person chooses to act virtuously, he does so for the sake of the "kalon"—a word that can mean "beautiful", "noble", or "fine" (SEP). The Greek philosopher believed in a soul and the gods, yet wisdom was the process and the pinnacle of a good life. As with the Dalai Lama, present-world thinkers find the search for the most noble and excellent qualities of life a worthy endeavor.

10
Disturbing Disruptions/Insightful Interruptions

My wife Carol was giving the Sunday morning message in a local congregation. Someone's phone began to ring. Carol smiled but continued. A short while later, the phone rang loudly once more. This time, Carol stopped and asked the woman if she needed help. A Black woman in another pew offered to help the older white woman. Carol's good at this; she asked the woman and the congregation: "how we can help." Assured the phone was off, the sermon moved on until, yes, it happened again. This time the woman got up and said she would take the phone out to her car. As she exited her pew, she responded to Carol's question about "inner work," confessing she talks too much and listens too little. There was laughter and nodding in empathetic support of this admission, as it seemed many of us were feeling the message of "inner work" applied to each of us.

When the unexpected breaks into our comfortable spaces—a noise, a voice, an action interrupts—the disturbance can be a wake up; we are startled into considering there may be something else that is happening, or needs to happen. In some cases, there is a shift, attention is transferred from what we thought was the central point or meaning to something potentially more meaningful and profound.

Consider the word "disruption," defined as "disturbance or problems which interrupt an event, activity, or process." According to the thesaurus we read: "disturbance, disordering, disarrangement, disarranging, interference, upset, upsetting, unsettling, confusion, confusing; disorderliness, disorganization, turmoil, disarray; interruption." Each of these descriptions can cause a confusing shake-up in our emotions. We may have to shift in a moment's time from feeling comfortable, settled, orderly, to complete disruption. The disturbance is ... disturbing!

I remember one Sunday years ago, the Black pastor of our ethnically diverse church was in the middle of his sermon when a bearded white man in the center of the sanctuary raised his voice to interject his opinion. Rev. Noel stopped, looked down at the man and said, firmly yet gently: "Jim, this is *my* time to speak. We'll hear from *you* later." The ladies sitting on either side of Jim nudged closer and whispered: "hush now, Jim." It was a memorable moment, especially when I later learned that many knew Jim, aware that he was "troubled" and lived outside. The sensitive way this 20-second disruption occurred helped shape my sense of what "church" and "ministry" truly mean. Disturbance cuts across lines, of gender, ethnicity, economic conditions, mental conditions and more. That is, if we allow the disruptive disturbances to be opportunities for insightful interruption.

Our street chaplaincy held gatherings in the free dining room downtown. I often asked our seminary interns to lead these circles consisting of "unhoused humans," community members including local clergy, and anyone who wandered in the open door off the street. One particular afternoon our intern John decided to read a children's book to the group. He thought it had a good message that would foster a helpful conversation. I told him beforehand it was risky; some may consider it condescending. Yet, I knew it would be a teaching moment for him and perhaps for the whole group. As he began to read and show the pictures—of an old wise turtle—a woman named Holly grew angry. She was our most volatile member. A resident of a nearby apartment building run by a mental health agency, it was clear from her dress and speech she was intelligent while easily agitated. Holly stood, shoved her chair, and yelled at John, making clear that she felt insulted he would read a child's story to adults. Storming out and slamming the door was of course very disturbing. The whole atmosphere of the group changed. After a stunned silence and deep breaths, we listened as a few shared Holly's dislike for the presentation and others expressed appreciation for John's leadership and the positive intent of the story. Some were critical of Holly and thought she shouldn't have been so disruptive.

We were tolerant to an extent with Holly and others who could be disruptive. A sense of safe sanctuary is important to protect, as is a peaceful classroom or community. Yet, in our best moments, we kept in mind that our intent, our plans, and our feelings, shouldn't always come first. We had to be prepared for the unexpected at any time to surprise us, disorient us, and maybe take us to a new level of understanding and empathy.

I'm the first to admit I don't exactly enjoy these "opportunities" for disturbing disruption. Though I've learned, with care and mindfulness, the ringing can wake us up to that inner work—a productive opportunity for insight.

11
Paul Laurence Dunbar & The Heart of Happy Hollow

Poet and novelist, Paul Laurence Dunbar (1872-1906), was born in Dayton, Ohio. His parents had been enslaved in Kentucky. According to the National Park Service that manages the Dunbar home in Dayton: "He was the only African American in the Central High School class of 1890" and Orville Wright was a classmate. Dunbar edited the school newspaper. Later, "Wright printed a newspaper that Paul published and edited for the African American community." In his 20's he befriended Frederick Douglass, who encouraged the young writer and he eventually became "the first African American to support himself financially through his writing."

I've been reading some of his short stories (though he only lived to be 33, he wrote four books of short stories). One tale in his collection, "The Heart of Happy Hollow," immediately captured my attention. In "Old Abe's Conversion" we're introduced to the Rev. Abram Dixon, a popular preacher who was excited to hear his son Robert was on a short leave from his own parish and coming home for a visit.

Abram had been a preacher on a plantation and never attended a seminary. "[He] had known no school except the fields where he had ploughed and sowed, the woods and the overhanging sky. He had sat under no teacher except the birds and the trees and the winds of heaven." He had "lived close to nature, and so, near to nature's God." The younger pastor tells his father that in his church: "we do a great deal in the way of charity work among the churchless and almost homeless city children." What the older pastor wants to know is how his son teaches "good strong doctern." Robert replies: "I try to tell them the truth as I see it and believe it. I try to hold up before them the right and the good and the clean and beautiful." Old pastor Dixon invites his son to preach in the hometown pulpit.

On Sunday morning, people were expecting the son to preach like the father. Instead, they thought he gave a dry lecture. Robert told his disappointed father he had done his best. A year went by and the elder Dixon came to Robert's town. The young minister walked with him by the streets and wharves where many youth were living in poverty. They entered a courtroom where a young boy stood before a judge who released him into Rev. Robert's care. As they walked out, the elder pastor asked the boy why he stole, and he replied: "I was hungry." Old pastor Dixon was moved. Then, after observing his son lead a group of rowdy youth at the church, he is convinced his son is doing good. He holds his son's hand and says: "I didn't understand."

At the Sunday service, the elder pastor Dixon was introduced before the congregation. He spoke of his conceit and the lessons he had learned from his son. "Why, people, I feels like a new convert!" The story concludes: "It was a gentler gospel than he had ever preached before, and in the congregation there were many eyes as wet as his own."

Paul Dunbar seemed sensitive to the tendencies of placing expectations on ministry. Could living among people in need and caring for them be as important as preaching? The father's congregation expected a stirring, entertaining, message. The younger minister was more interested in engaging action and a presence of compassion than in words and preaching.

One of Dunbar's most famous poems, "Sympathy," provided the title to Maya Angelou's autobiography, "I Know Why the Caged Bird Sings":

"I know what the caged bird feels, alas!

>   When the sun is bright on the upland slopes;
> When the wind stirs soft through the springing grass,
> And the river flows like a stream of glass;
>   When the first bird sings and the first bud opes,
> And the faint perfume from its chalice steals—
> I know what the caged bird feels!
>
> . . .
>
> I know why the caged bird sings, ah me,
>   When his wing is bruised and his bosom sore,—
> When he beats his bars and he would be free;
> It is not a carol of joy or glee,
>   But a prayer that he sends from his heart's deep core,
> But a plea, that upward to Heaven he flings—
> I know why the caged bird sings!"

Robert was able to spread his wings, to get an education and find his own way, his own ministry among the poorest in his community. Though his father believed he knew what ministry meant, he found a new, humbler voice. He had forgotten he once had teachers among the fields, trees and birds. His conversion opened the cage and made him sing.

12
The Devil's in the Details: Do We Still Need Satan?

During summer hot spells, my mother used to say it's "hotter than the hubs of Hades." Heat can be hellish. So can our beliefs.

When you imagine "the Face of Evil" I would guess it has a human face. Does a world leader appear? Does your mind conjure up a picture of something in a film or book, or a frightening creature described in a sermon or a painting on a Sunday School wall?

"Evil" is (lazy) shorthand for the worst actions of people, or the people themselves. When I was a chaplain, entering seven separate units of a county jail every week for ten years, I met with men and women who were called "evil" or "monsters" out in the public or in newspapers. Learning their names, looking in their eyes, hearing their stories, shaking hands or hugging them, I saw each individual as a deeply troubled human being, not inhuman, evil or monstrous.

As for the monstrosity some traditions call "Satan," I think we're merely putting a face and a name on something or someone we fear or fail to understand. A natural phobia of the unknown morphs into a belief in something beyond the human, something super-natural. People think they know what the Bible teaches about this character, but I wonder. "In Hebrew, the term Satan is usually translated as 'opponent' or 'adversary,' and he is often understood to represent the sinful impulse or, more generally, the forces that prevent human beings from submitting to divine will" (www.myjewishlearning.com). This personification (anthropomorphic evil) is opposed to God's way, yet needs divine permission to do anything to anyone. A strange image, though religions often provide a tempting alternative to faithfulness, otherwise there would be nothing to compare to—or challenge—the good and righteous path.

Christian tradition has run wild with the concept, creating a kind of sinister anti-superhero called the devil (diabolos in Greek). The legendary tale of "Lucifer" who "fell from heaven" is one odd story squeezed from an ancient text (Isaiah) that has nothing to do with our modern superstitions of Satan. For those of us raised in Sunday School we remember the terrible tale of Job (not the best bedtime story). God allows a shadowy fellow named "the satan" to do all kinds of awful things to test the faith of an innocent man—really quite cruel and unfair. But who was this persecutor sent by God? A meanspirited prosecutor who accused Job and then was given permission from the Judge to do anything but kill him. This raises a whole courtroom full of ethical and theological questions. What kind of judge—or god—would allow such a tortuous test?

"The Jewish mystical tradition has much to say about Satan ... and the demonic realm [but] on the whole, Satan occupies a far more prominent place in Christian theology than in traditional rabbinic sources" (www.myjewishlearning.com). Satan tempting Jesus in the desert, then falling out of heaven in defeat (Luke 10; John 12—then somehow directing cosmic wars in the Book of Revelation)—these are images burned into the minds of orthodox and folk traditions that felt the need to have a mythological opponent to God's vulnerable people. "Some of these Christian ideas are echoed in Jewish tradition, but some also point to fundamental differences — most notably perhaps the idea that, in the Hebrew Bible at least, Satan is ultimately subordinate to God, carrying out his purpose on earth. Or that he isn't real at all, but is merely a metaphor for sinful impulses" (www.myjewishlearning.com).

The plea in the Lord's Prayer, "Lead us not into temptation," relates to this ancient idea that the gods need an opponent, so a satan figure is created to tempt and test humans so they will cling to a God who will "deliver us from evil." Early Christians believed they were in the center of a cosmic war, persecuted by malevolent forces. It was not always clear who was winning, who the real Ruler of the World actually was.

Most of our scary images and feelings about Satan and the Devil come not from the Bible but from our most fantastical imaginations. As children we learn to fear the "Dark Lord" Vader in Star Wars, Lord Voldemort in Harry Potter, Sauron in Lord of the Rings—all sorts of nasty evildoers and shadowy creatures. The forces of Good always win the day and we're relieved—at least until the next fantasy film.

A contemporary example of the creative use of the adversarial nature of the Satan image is the work of The Satanic Temple, whose seven "Fundamental Tenets" emphasize compassion, justice, respect for personal freedoms, science and wisdom, because they believe "Satan is a symbol of the Eternal Rebel in opposition to arbitrary authority."

We may claim "the devil made me do it," or enjoy "playing devil's advocate" with a "devil-may-care" attitude, but truth is, we may need a little more satan sometimes.

13
If We Applied Our Minds to Know Wisdom

> "I applied my mind to know wisdom..."
> Koheleth, 1:13, 17; 8:16

Not applied to know "God" or "be religious" or have more faith. Wisdom is enough. But hold it in your hands and it drips away like water, or honey. Fill your head and it's empty. Spend your life seeking for answers, solutions, conclusions and you end up with a basket-full of questions and conundrums. It's all a "chasing after wind," which could be translated "feeding on wind" or, as I think of it: "taking lots of long, deep breaths" or even "gasping for air." We feel breathless.

The writer of Koheleth was, as one of my students described him, having an "existential crisis." To say he was perplexed and puzzled by the paradoxes all around him would be paltry. Discouraged, depressed, down-hearted by the world around him, whoever this teacher was, he sure wanted some answers.

Who or what is the Breath-giver, this "god" whose action and inaction bewilders Koheleth? The best response may be to keep searching, questioning, wondering.

Wisdom is not a destination. Wisdom is a search, perhaps the most important search. Like knowledge, we keep learning. Each step taken, every door opened, presents a bigger picture. Yet, no one can truly see the larger view, The Big Picture always will be out of reach, just beyond the stretch of our legs, arms and brains.

The goal is wisdom, sound judgement, useful knowledge, practical information. The goal is not faith, or religion or god. Not even happiness or complete understanding. My college major in Philosophy and Religion inspired that interest in pursuing wisdom. . .a determined, decisive practice of searching for wisdom. And just because something is called "wisdom literature" or a person is called "wise" doesn't make it so. Wisdom, like ethical teachings, can come from anywhere, anyplace, anyone at anytime.

In college days my newly awakened thrill with everything wise took Proverbs seriously: "Get wisdom." Whatever you do, whatever you believe, get some, and get it now!

We might disagree on some interpretations or readings of the texts, but the goal is to get a better grasp on the practical meaning of what we read. That's wisdom: knowing how to apply what we learn from our experience, to our lives. Whether our teacher is Koheleth of Jerusalem or Jesus of Nazareth, they had to do their own search and study in the Book of Life, to learn the practice of wisdom. Then, like any competent instructor, they each sought to pass along practical knowledge: they were *wise human beings teaching us how to be wise human beings.* Teachers teaching us how to teach ourselves.

We may find the answers, the most significant, meaningful and ultimate conclusions are (as irritating as it is) questions. Koheleth was caught in a web, some of that woven by himself. The teacher was caught in a web of paradoxes. This is how I outlined that web for my class:

Pregnant Paradoxes and Drumming Conundrums in Koheleth

Creative Contradictions
(Good/Evil, Life/Death, Wise/Foolish, etc)

Making Sense of Nonsense
(Be wise enough to know wisdom can be useless)

Seeking to Know the Unknowable
(Search for what can't be found)

Meaning in the Meaningless
(Enjoy life, though there is suffering; make your own

meaning, though there is none)

The Breath-giver has a Strategy but we'll never know what it is
(If you think you know what the Creator is doing, you don't)

The heartbeat of philosophical ("spiritual") struggles
(The Teacher is wrestling with himself, the world, his "God")

My book, *Breath, Death and Koheleth*, opens with a quote from Rabbi Levi Yitzhak: "In reality, not only the black letters but the while gaps in between, are symbols of the teaching, only that we are not able to read those gaps." Brilliant. The good rabbi speaks the paradoxical language of Koheleth, pointing to the teachings that are not found on the page.
- What's NOT being said?
- What's in the margins?
- Look behind the words on the page
- Build on Questions, the wonder
- Be a Skeptic

Kind of a holy confusion, perhaps?

A mental exercise I like to play—*What if all we had for scripture or ancient wisdom tradition was Koheleth?* This one book was our One Book. If we were thinking of creating a new religion or ethical practice based solely on Koheleth, what would that new religious practice or lifestyle be? What would the essential principles be? What would that look like? Could we find any followers?!

14
Do Different Paths Lead to the Same Peak?

We hiked up a Forest Service road near Pisgah Inn to reach the fire lookout on Frying Pan mountain. Nothing was frying, though we did see a burned-out firepit and the Forest Service employee wasn't amused by my suggestion we swap stories around the campfire (in fact, there was a wild fire nearby a few weeks later). It was a breezy spring afternoon when we climbed as high as our stomachs could handle on the swaying stairs. The view was spectacular but we were grateful for solid ground when we descended.

We were almost back to the car when I noticed an unmarked trail branching off to the left. Thinking it might be a short dead-end, we were pleased to find that it wound through the forest near a stream. One of our favorite kinds of paths—no sign and no sign of anyone else. Another brief adventure in our explorations along the Blue Ridge.

Over dinner we arrived at the same conclusion: there is always another trail. Not simply an acknowledgment there are numerous trails to explore in these mountains, we were expressing the enjoyment we feel each time we make plans for one destination and discover a branching opportunity, an alternative direction to an unknown place, or places.

During my years of inter-religious work, one guiding image was the analogy of the "many paths up the mountain." It seemed reasonable to frame all religions and hence all "spiritual travelers" as different paths or pathfinders leading to the same goal: enlightenment, salvation, union with God, whatever that notion of God was in various traditions. Now, I wonder if this pretty picture is much too simplistic, unhelpful and perhaps unhealthy. Maybe a nice idea for some, but not accurate or honest. It's simply not true.

Do all paths lead to the same place? Think of those trails, all the trails and pathways across different lands, in the mountains, through various forests, along rivers, on ocean shores, winding through deserts. Do they all intersect at some imagined point, at some imagined "Person" called god or goddess? In my mind, this way of thinking is not what religion or faith means or even intends.

In his opening speech at the first Parliament of Religions held in Chicago in 1893, Hindu teacher Swami Vivekananda declared: "The present convention ... is in itself a vindication, a declaration to the world, of the wonderful doctrine preached in [Hindu scripture]: 'Whosoever comes to Me, through whatsoever form, I reach him; all men are struggling through paths which in the end lead to Me.'" I can appreciate that sentiment, but I no longer consider it a useful way to think of religion or honestly practice a faith.

When we explore an unknown trail, curious and open to what we may find along the way, it's possible we will see, hear and touch many things others have also seen, heard and touched. Depending on our attentiveness, chances are we will experience some things never experienced by anyone: a new species, a fresh rivulet following a rainstorm, a mix of living things and images that paint a picture no one has ever seen. And we may be standing right in it, a part of the painting. A wild moment of participation in the environment. If we choose to tell the story of what we've walked into, there may be similarities with descriptions from others near or far. Yet, it will never truly be the same.

There are rich tales from many traditions of people encountering something or someone on a newly discovered path. Some climb a mountain and say they spoke with a deity; others sail the seas and relate "divine encounters"; and some sit in a quiet forest and "commune with god." These can be quite profound for an individual and may even lead to the birth of a religion. Could we say these diverse experiences and the beliefs they stir share a common or an identical goal or intent? I would agree there may certainly be a shared intention: to feel in relation to something greater. Concerning belief systems, the origin of religions, I would have to say each one establishes their own unique path. In a sense, every religion paves its own trail believing it is the "best" or "only" way. Each trail claims it is, in itself, the goal, the destination, the peak. We end up with the mishmash hinted at by Vivekananda whose very framing of unity exposes a sectarian perspective: one central scripture from one central tradition proclaiming all paths lead to one main deity: his—Krishna.

There is always another trail beckoning beyond. The delight is in the discovery of the unnamed, unsigned, perhaps unexplored paths.

15
The Thinking Earth & the Laughing Tree

In her memorable and moving story, "John Redding Goes to Sea," Zora Neale Hurston draws the reader into a lingering tension within a family living off the land in Florida. Ten-year-old John is an odd child who wanders alone to the river, dreaming of lands far away. John is described as "puzzling to the simple folk there in the Florida woods." Though his mother wonders if her son is "conjured" with a spell of some kind, his father doesn't want the boy to get that "foolishness" in his head. The dreamy kid has unusual thoughts but his father insists his wife can believe what she wants to but she shouldn't tell John any of it.

When John takes his walks through the woods near

the river, he is troubled by one old twisted tree that resembles a skull; at sunset it makes him sad and scared. At times John imagines the strange tree laughs at him. When he tells his sympathetic father, the response comes in tender, common language: "Yuh wuz always imagin 'things, John, things that nobody else evah thought on!" The boy grows contemplative, expressing his feelings of being trapped in that place using images from his immediate environment. He says: "Sometimes I feel that I am just earth, 'soil 'lying helpless to move myself, but 'thinking'." He senses herds of animals running above him, rain and wind washing over him. These are "all acting upon me, but me, well, just soil, 'feeling 'but not able to take part in it all." It's not all bad, however. He also feels a warming love in summer showers that "softens" him: "I push a blade of grass or a flower, or maybe a pine tree—that's the ground thinking." His natural and childlike imagination carries his mind deeper: "Plants are ground thoughts, because the soil can't move itself." He knows he's a dreamer, but he has "such wonderfully complete dreams [that] never come true. But even as my dreams fade I have others."

The beauty of these words has a certain glow to it, like a spring night by a slow river.

John's mother, Maddy, thinks it's crazy talk that her boy wants to go to distant lands. She's frightened at the thought he would leave. Her anger and tears convince him to stay longer, but eventually he goes to school and gets married before choosing to join the Navy and go the way of his dreams. His mother can't understand "why he should wish to go strange places where neither she nor his father had been." No one had ever gone far from the village. They wanted John to stay and teach school. His mother refuses to give her consent for his travels. John pleads: "What is there here for me? Why, sometimes I get to feeling just like a lump of dirt turned over by the plow ... no thought or movement or nothing."

After John tells his father of his feelings of being "just earth," the older man replies: "Yas, son, Ah have them same feelings exactly, but Ah can't find no words lak you do. It seems lak you an 'me see wid de same eyes, hear wid de same ears an 'even feel de same inside. Only thing you kin talk it an 'Ah can't. But anyhow you speaks for me, so what's the difference?"

"John Redding Goes to Sea" was Hurston's first published story, appearing in 1921. I won't give away the surprising conclusion to this short story (Alice Walker said it made her cry, for sorrow and joy), but you might say John achieves his dream.

In 1960, Zora Neale Hurston died in a segregated "welfare home" (of a stroke and possibly malnutrition) and was buried in an unmarked grave in Florida. Alice Walker found that cemetery and the gravesite to make sure Hurston was honored, placing a marker on her place of rest. Walker wrote: "There are times—and finding Zora Hurston's grave was one of them—when normal responses of grief, horror, and so on, do not make sense because they bear no real relation to the depth of the emotion one feels" ("In Search of Zora Neale Hurston").

One can't help reflecting on Hurston's life and death as a touch of what that old tree was laughing about. To be buried near her childhood home but mostly unknown, forgotten, neglected. Alice Walker tried to change that by marking her grave. Yet, what do we do with dreamy storytellers like Zora Hurston and John Redding? They are of the earth but seek to be more than soil, ground, compost. It may be the fact they "push a blade of grass or a flower, or maybe a pine tree," they become "the ground thinking." And so their lives are plowed and planted for a harvest of dreams again.

16
**Three Mothers, Three Preachers,
Three Transformative Sons**

Louise Little, Alberta King, Berdis Baldwin. Three strong Black women, each married to a preacher; each the mother of a man who preached … and changed history. Their sons raised their voices for racial equality and fundamental human rights: Malcolm X, Martin Luther King, Jr., and James Baldwin.

In her book, *The Three Mothers*, Anna Malaika Tubbs writes: "Each woman was already living an incredible life that her children would one day follow. Their identities as young Black girls in Georgia, Grenada and Maryland influenced the ways in which they would approach motherhood. Their exposure to racist and sexist violence from the moment they were born would inform the lessons they taught their children." These women were persistent and resistant to those who would keep them down, in their "place," as women, as Black women.

"They found ways to give life and to humanize themselves, their children, and in turn, our entire community. As history tells us, all of their sons did indeed make a difference in this world, but they did so at a cost. In all three cases, the mothers 'worst fears became reality: each woman was alive to bury her son." Many Black mothers, and grandmothers, still do.

Anna Tubbs refers to the analogy of a crooked room (borrowed from Melissa Harris-Perry). In an experiment, people sat in a crooked chair in a crooked room and when asked to sit up straight, they still leaned over, feeling they were sitting straight when aligned with other objects in the room. A connection is made to the pressure on Black women to conform to the alignment of society's expectations—they "find it hard to stand up straight in a crooked room." As Tubbs makes the connection to Louise, Alberta and Berdis, the crooked rooms changed during their lives as they got out of their chairs, stood tall, and rearranged rooms, helping straighten them for others. Such a useful image for the many ways communities, including religious communities, pressure people to conform, to "sit up straight" and accept the tilted worldview they are presented. Given that each of these mothers married a preacher whose flaws or fragility proved harmful to the family, it's remarkable to see the leadership emerge—strong males who found deep strength in their mothers who passed on their upright and righteous gifts.

One description of Louise Little's parenting style and the way it helped shape Malcolm's outlook is remarkable. Reading and writing were high expectations—a dictionary was always near at hand—but so was an eclectic exposure to diverse religious beliefs: "She didn't subscribe to one particular religion but instead wanted to expose her children to several different faiths. She took her children everywhere: they attended Catholic mass, congregated with Baptists, and learned from Hindus." As someone committed to education, Louise made sure when they came home from these religious gatherings they would talk about what they learned and ask questions. She would tell them: "You take what you see will fit you, and the rest of it, just leave it there." In her mind it was more important to have a relationship with the Creator than to be confused by so many traditions, to get "hung up in these religions." The year before his assassination in 1965, Malcolm made the Hajj, the journey to Mecca. His experience was shaped by his Muslim faith, and by his mother's early lessons that taught him people of many colors and religions can be brothers and sisters.

While Martin was in seminary he wrote to his mother: "I often tell the boys around campus I have the best mother in the world." Alberta King's strength and guidance deeply influenced Martin and her voice can be heard in his sense of ministry: "Any religion that professes concern for the souls of men and is not equally concerned about the slums that damn them, the economic conditions that strangle them, and the social conditions that cripple them is a spiritually moribund religion only waiting for the day to be buried."

Berdis Baldwin was consistently encouraging and supportive of her son Jimmy. In his life and writing he wanted people to know his mother deserved credit and "that everyone would gain more knowledge if Berdis were asked to share her wisdom after all she'd witnessed." At her son's memorial in 1987, the sanctuary at St. John the Divine in New York City was filled with her cries. As with each of these influential mothers, the cord of connection was powerful.

Near the conclusion of her book on the three mothers, Anna Tubbs writes: "They did not write books ... they cared more about passing on their lessons." Now, we read the books of their sons, and hear the heartbeat of their courageous mothers.

17
A Sticky Note in the Wind or on the Breath

Brainshower thought: I'm constantly handling, sometimes dropping, these slippery terms used for the things we believe in. Often the words we reach for are perhaps more sticky than slippery. They stick to us or stick in our minds. Hard to shake.

I've been pondering if the word, the concept, the idea, the name "God" could be something we write on a mental sticky note to adhere to the wind, even our breath?

Contemplating these things brings me to a thought I had just before turning off the lamp the other night. I was reading the story of an enslaved person in 18th C. England who was told he was going to hell unless he was baptized. Can you guess the choice he made? Frightened by punishment beyond the grave, he was baptized in London by a clergyperson apparently unperturbed by slavery. Salvation—freedom in Christ—was paramount. What came to mind as I switched off the light was how we read people, or books, or the world around us, with particular eyes. What I jotted down on the nightstand was: "To read something with Christian eyes is to Christianize what is being read." It may be unconscious, but we place our own meaning and interpretation on something, like a story, for instance.

This enslaved man was kidnapped from his village in Africa, torn from his family, and became the property of an Englishman. Over the next few years, he learned to dress and speak like his master, then to be baptized to believe the same. I reasoned that some people reading his narrative might be pleased to hear this young man's description of becoming "more English" (i.e., more civilized and christianized). They might read this story through the eyes of a Christian—a religious perspective—and thereby "christianize" the narrative.

How does this relate to sticky notes? I wondered if you'd ask. It's a fairly simple question: Are we human beings predisposed to "religionize" things, the world? We don't understand something or can't see something so we write a label on a note and make the attempt to make it stick—to something, like veritable velcro. Koheleth (Ecclesiastes, the Teacher) applied his mind to grasp what is going on "under the sun" and felt it was all futile, an empty "chasing after wind" (or gasping for air). We might feel that sense sometimes ourselves. So we try to stick some sense on our hopes, our imagination or plain nonsense claiming to know the unknowable—or at least name it.

Once again I'm adhering to a sticky situation.

18
The Sweetness of Light in the Blink of an Eye

In the biblical book of Koheleth (Ecclesiastes), we read: "Light is sweet." When we read this in a class I was teaching, someone said it should be "life is sweet." That's what we're used to hearing, but many scriptures of the world speak of light, enlightenment, the sun. Jesus is called "the Light of the World," yet says his followers are "the light of the world." And we're told by some traditions that darkness, like death, is to be feared, though we all face it someday. Additionally, some are encouraged to "turn a blind eye" to some offense or distraction. Blindness is used as a lesson in spiritual matters. We never want to lose our sight; light is sweet.

At the conclusion of another class, a bright flash

crossed my left eye. When I got home I thought something was in my eye but drops didn't help. Then I saw there were dark floating strands moving around inside my eyeball. Alarmed, I told my wife and then called for an emergency appointment with the eye doctor. In an exam the next day, the ophthalmologist calmly told me I had "floaters"—vitreous fluid or cell debris in my field of vision. "Comes with age," she assured me. I didn't feel very assured. This came on so suddenly and I wasn't at all convinced I would "get used to it."

How do we handle these instantaneous moments in life when something profoundly changes? What do we do when a physical issue, mental alteration, or a change in relationship, job or a death occurs? It can make us feel fragile, vulnerable and perhaps frightened. And it can all happen in the wink of a second, in the blink of an eye.

A story I've told many times concerns the trailwork I did while living on an island in the Pacific Northwest. All alone deep in the woods I was clearing brush when a small branch poked me in the eye. Not sure if I'd actually lost my eye, I stumbled back to my tiny cabin with intense pain. Gently washing the area I finally got the courage to look in a mirror. Relieved to see I still had my eye, I kept it covered for several days. Gratefully recovering one afternoon, I continued to squint, guarding my injury, while walking out to my compost. Something caught my attention in the alder above me. My feathery neighbor the barred owl was staring down at me. I almost thought I was dreaming. She had one eye closed. The same one I injured!

"The eye is the lamp of the body. So, if your eye is healthy your whole body will be full of light" (Matthew 6). I think I understand the meaning here, yet the eye is not the lamp—it allows light to enter the body. If you are "dark inside" then you need to find ways of letting in the light. We could have long discussions how to do that. Some say faith is the light. Others say reason. Sometimes perhaps a combination. Yet the point is fairly clear: get light! (Jesus probably didn't mean light-headed though).

The Hindu "Gita" speaks of "the inner light." Mystics have always used this language. Having "the eyes to see" is a practice of opening windows of perception, or kindling a hidden lamp within. For these folks, the senses are like symbols for something "deeper" yet brighter. The "Tao Te Ching" says: "The sage regards their center, and not their eyes" (12). Gautama Buddha taught: "In the midst of blind mortals, the truly enlightened shine" (Dhammapada 4:16). Yet, some caution is in order. Those who claim to see, hear, feel or touch something or someone "beyond the senses" can't be disproved or even questioned. Freethinkers will always question and hold high the essential lamp of reason. The Roman Stoic Epictetus wrote: "most of you are blinded." For the philosopher, the cure is wisdom, practical knowledge applied with all senses fully functional, especially common sense.

All this is not to say there are no moments when a flash of light crosses our vision. What happened to me after that class could be interpreted as a "message," a glimpse of enlightenment. Well, no, possibly the beginning of a cataract (and a disturbing sign of aging), but I experienced no new "insights" other than the fact that many others live with "floaters" too.

The writer of Koheleth claimed he saw "nothing new under the sun." Hard to see how he missed it. When we most appreciate our sight, when we are truly grateful for these amazing organs we call eyes, everything is new under the sun, in the light, the sweet light, of day.

19
The Elimination of the Unthinkable

Here's a rather crude exercise to begin a serious discussion of worthiness, greatness or perhaps saintliness—one quick way to consider those we most highly esteem.

Think of a person you greatly admire or revere in history. They could be a political leader, a religious teacher or other respected person. It could even be a sports figure or entertainer held high as an icon. Now, have a vivid image of them in mind.

Ok, now here's the hard part that may deeply offend some. Imagine that person right now in a bathroom, seated on the toilet. No doubt this will be difficult and you may quickly dismiss that picture in your mind.

Never something we want to think about. No one wants to talk about it because it's uncomfortable or simply "unthinkable."

Some years ago I wrote a little ditty, a light and lilting song that can be sung as a kind of jingle. Think of it as a Monty Python-style musical sketch. The piece began with the words: "Everybody has to eliminate, no matter if you're po 'or a potentate." It made me laugh, but I don't think I ever sang the song to anyone, though it felt liberating to me. The whole—or "hole"—image reminded me of something a friend told me in high school. I was ogling a popular sweet and cute Christian singer and he said: "She has to sit on the pot just like us." I gave a nervous laugh, but loved it. A quick, down-to-earth way of remembering we are all human no matter the pedestal we place some fellow human beings upon (the pedestal never seems to have a hole in it). The famous and infamous, the great and the small, the known and the unknown—in whatever position we hold in life, we're in it, and sit it, together.

In a seminary course on Christian scriptures, we were assigned a book that, among other radical concepts, suggested we think of humans as "gods with anuses" (Ernst Becker, *The Denial of Death*). We all thought that was humorous, yet, upon reflection, we found it a statement of troubling truth. Though the Psalms and Jesus himself say "we are as gods," Christian tradition has virtually ignored that. How can we be divine when we're just so ... human?

Yet, the Jesus Story is lifted up as a powerful presentation of the Human-God unity. The holy and divine descends to the dirty, sinful earth to become a superhero savior who, oddly enough, never seems to get dirty. At least this is the enduring and endearing image of him. Though born in a cattle feeding trough, dying nailed to a bloody tree, and buried in a muddy hole in the ground, the story ignores 18 years of his life in the filth of humanity and can't wait to raise him from the corruption of death to get back up to the pure world above.

In the 1990's, while delving into the "Men's Movement," I read a book entitled, "A Choice of Heroes." In American culture, boys are raised with many choices when it comes to models or examples of manhood. Military leaders, movie stars and sports figures dominate the field. When I think back to boyhood, I can almost laugh out loud. Many of my "great men" were fictional, cartoonish superhero kinds of males. Oddly, but perhaps not surprisingly, in my teen years Jesus of Nazareth became a paragon of what it meant to be a "real man." Tough, yet tender, vulnerable yet victorious. Yet, ultimately he was unworldly, not fully human, not like me; not actually a real man at all.

The strange history of the Church holds their Christ high as the paramount person, the best model for being human, the epitome of humanity, all the while holding him so high he could never be a serious, practical model for living (consider the doctrine that he was "without sin," or the unspoken belief he never had sexual relations). He was forever out of reach of mere mortals, nearly floating as a ghostly presence across the Judean landscape. In my later Christian years, particularly in ministry, the men (and women) I most respected were Civil Rights leaders and elected representatives who stood for the highest ideals of an inclusive community, placing the poor foremost in faithful concern or social action. Though some might have believed Jesus was a guiding presence in their lives, I was most impressed that these contemporary leaders practiced his basic ethical teachings, not that they were believing Christians.

Jesus had to go. I mean, literally, he had to go to the bathroom, or equivalent in his day. As an itinerant preacher, he would have had to "go" in the woods, fields, hills, behind a barn. Why has someone never told a story of flowers sprouting from his waste or a miracle of healing from a person touching his pee? This is, I'm sure, too much—a bridge, or bathroom, too far—for most, especially those who hold him so high and pure he could never be made "impure" by doing something so natural, earthy, human. Yet, in my view, this must be something as contemplated by believers as any other aspect of his life. In the context of their lord squatting over a hole or on a crude commode, the full and inglorious humanity of the holy hero takes on a new quality that resists ripping asunder the sacred and secular. As I see it, as I understand it, Jesus was completely secular because he was as human as anyone. For this I think he can be honored by non-believers as well as believers.

I'm not suggesting Jesus of Nazareth is the only revered teacher in religious history who needs to be re-humanized. Buddha had to squat in the forest, Moses on Sinai, Muhammad in his Arabian cave. Each and all were made of the stuff we are all made of and returned to the humus that receives us all. Their gift to humanity wasn't their super-humanity but their radical embodiment of what it means to be breathing flesh that includes the same messiness that makes us who we are.

Once again, the reason for my treading into this taboo territory (careful of what I may step on) is to open up serious discussion on this touchy issue of veneration. It's the most natural thing for religious beliefs to shun the most natural things, to substitute the super-natural so as to slip around the thought or admission their godly hero was a real human being (for example, the way Jesus became the Christ in the early Church). To venerate is to adore and to adore means to worship and pray to someone. A "person" we pray to and worship can never be seen as too human since we can't imagine venerating someone who truly and completely shares our humanness. The dilemma faith must face is how to venerate a god in human form, a god who digests and creates waste, a god who never quite fits in human skin.

The faith community can no longer avoid the

"voiding" (sorry, but it's not easy to step around this s*#t). This is a subject, however uncomfortable, that can't be left to rest in the restroom. It doesn't sit right for some of us. We humans think we're pretty great—and, truth is, we are. Godlike beings, we're also fragile, frail and flawed. That is greatness. And true greatness is seeing this, admitting it, and standing tall, or sitting proud … even in what we euphemistically call, the "washroom."

20
**The Coffin Confessor
& Doing Something We Have to Do**

One of my favorite podcasts is "This American Life." A recent episode was a string of stories on the theme: "Well, Someone Had to Do Something!" A man in Seattle picks up a stranger's stolen bike from thieves who listed it on Craigslist. He takes this risky action for many others, simply for the satisfaction and appreciation. Polish families leave strollers at a train station for arriving Ukrainians. A Lithuanian man sets up a website for Russian-speaking expatriots to call random households in Russia to explain the realities of the war. Staff in a Ukrainian zoo move their families inside to care for the animals during the conflict. One even sleeps in with an elephant sensitive to nearby explosions.

Hearing these stories of people doing extraordinary things in extraordinary circumstances is both emotional and inspiring. We see the height of humanity in the midst of inhumanity. Responding in the face of fear, when crime and war expose the best and worst of our world, is a powerful testimony to our ability to do amazing things, or simply do what must be done, in the name of our highest ideals. People step up to help by stepping into the tension, terror and turmoil that potentially cause us to give up and give in to our fear or despair.

On the podcast we hear the story of the "Coffin Confessor," a man who was asked to read a eulogy written by someone who was dying. After the man passed away, his "confessor" stood to read the words in the memorial service. Some were startled and upset by the pointed remarks to family and friends, blunt words the dying man chose not to confront them with in life. Others thanked him for reading the eulogy and word got out what he had done. He became known as the "Coffin Confessor," often requested to perform this risky, uncomfortable task. One tattooed biker guy wrote in his eulogy that he was gay though he hadn't told anyone. Those who attended his service were surprised but it felt liberating to speak, and hear, the honest truth the biker was hesitant to reveal.

"This American Life" opens the door to invite our own humanity to come out and flourish, to be seen, heard and felt. We constantly see the low-water marks of our nature, the "ethical drought" in a threatening world, so it's good to show the high-water marks as well. In many instances, it's our free choice to "go low" or "go high." Our worldview, our sense of where we fit in the larger picture, can make all the difference how we act, how we respond to the heights and depths, the best and worst of society. Overwhelmed with a barrage of information that may or may not contain truthful and useful knowledge, we need to ask ourselves: Do we possess a fundamental wisdom to discern what is good and right for ourselves and others? The Roman Stoic philosopher Lucius Seneca wrote: "The first thing philosophy promises us is the feeling of fellowship, of belonging to [humankind] and being members of a community" (Letter V). The pursuit of wisdom is no dry, detached endeavor; it is a wise search for what may be best for our community. The philosopher of nature, Henry Thoreau, was on his deathbed when, it is reported, a pastor asked if he could see the promised land. Henry drew a long breath and replied: "One world at a time." If only this sense and sensibility could be practiced by more people of faith. If we are distracted by narrow, parochial thinking, we imagine an American life is more valuable than any other life, that another world is what really matters, not the messy, uncomfortable, challenging world we face here, now, together.

When we turn to the Wisdom Traditions of the world, religions or philosophical outlooks, what are we seeking and for what purpose? Is it for a relation with something beyond the human, or a way to live well? How might we step up to speak truth, to be "confessors" revealing what others may not feel free or safe to say? Leaving a stroller at a train station, anticipating the arrival of strangers in need, is a selfless act of conscience and compassion. Caring for and calming vulnerable animals are also very human—and humane—actions to take.

What do we have to confess? (keep in mind, this is not about confession of sins). What truths do we sense are necessary to bring to light? We resist confessing our true nature, and the nature of others, yet, we may be the "someone" to do something while others choose to stand silent.

21
Olaudah Equiano: Slave, Sailor, Scribe

Kidnapped from his Benin village in Africa when he was eleven (1756), Olaudah Equiano spent many years of his life enslaved. When he was finally given the opportunity to learn to read and write, he kept a record of his adventurous journeys, published in London in 1789 as *The Life of Olaudah Equiano*. His compelling storytelling made the book a bestseller.

Equiano uses the first part of his narrative to describe his early life in Africa. Years after his capture and enslavement his memory remained sharp. His village was far from the coast, in fact, he had: "never heard of white men or Europeans, nor of the sea." His father was a village elder and the family participated in memorable rituals and ceremonies as well as exchanges of slaves between tribes (the narrator makes it clear that slavery was only for prisoners of war and as punishment for serious crimes). "We are almost a nation of dancers, musicians, and poets," he writes, speaking with affection and in the present tense. The women of the village work in the fields like the men as well as spin, weave and dye clothing and make pottery and pipes. Growing crops was a central part of village life and everyone contributed and shared in the abundance. "We have no beggars," he explained.

Faith plays an important part in the story. Though he became a fervent Christian later, Equiano speaks with respect for the religious beliefs of his early years. "As to religion, the [African] natives believe that there is one Creator of all things, and that he lives in the sun." This Creator was the overseer of tribal life though Equiano remembered no discussion of an after-life except the belief that ancestors were near. Recalling his mother—"I was almost constantly with her"—he describes her offerings and laments, which as a small boy frightened him. At the time of his birth he was named "Olaudah" meaning "one favoured, and having a loud voice and well spoken." He honored the belief that the image of the Creator was "carved in ebony," and he was disturbed when Africans were among White people and forgot their "language, religion, manners and customs." Based on his own terrible experiences, he asks: "Are they treated as men? Does not slavery itself depress the mind, and extinguish all its fire ...? In this eloquent section, when the narrator puts White and Black beside each other on equal ground, he quotes an oft-forgotten passage from the Book of Acts: "God has made of one blood all nations of humanity to dwell on the face of the earth" (17:26).

The youngest of seven children, Olaudah was especially beloved by his mother who encouraged him to be a protector, a warrior. At the age of eleven he would climb a tree to watch over other village children while their parents were in the fields. One day kidnappers arrived and the children ran. Equiano and his sister were captured. He saw his sister one more time, but cruelly never saw his family again. He was taken aboard a slave ship bound for Barbados, then Virginia and on to England. He had several masters and captains on his many sea voyages through the years. Learning to read after thinking he could "talk to the books," he grew to be an essential part of any crew.

While serving in a London household, he was told he would not go to heaven unless he was baptized. Worried, he asked his master to take him to a priest for baptism, though it wasn't until some years later he overcame his "fear of eternity" and converted. Finally purchasing his freedom from his owner on Montserrat about 1766, he felt it was the happiest day of his life to become, as he powerfully states, "my own master."

The rest of his story reads somewhat like the miraculous shipboard tales of the Apostle Paul. Equiano has both tragic and inspiring experiences traveling as a free man. One passage shows his insatiable curiosity. While sailing the Mediterranean, he encountered Turks who were kind and honest, yet wouldn't allow him, as a Christian, into their mosques. This troubled Olaudah because he was "always fond of going to see the different modes of worship of the people wherever I went."

The final legacy of Equiano, along with his narrative, was the fight to end slavery. In 1788 he presented a petition to the Queen and continued to work with abolitionists until his death in 1797.

We purchased a copy of "The Life of Olaudah Equiano" at Fort Sumter, SC where the American war over slavery began. A powerfully significant place to discover one courageous human being's story of faith, freedom and fortitude.

22
**Preachers in Public Schools—
One Parent's Perfect Response**

When an athlete in a public high school relayed to her parents that a preacher from an Evangelical church was regularly coming to practice, preaching and praying with the team and coaches, the parents were upset. The next time the preacher came, one parent was in attendance and, wisely, recorded the incident.

This parent reached out to me, knowing I was a former minister and secular person with some knowledge of church/state separation issues. As a member of Americans United, the Freedom From Religion Foundation and the American Humanist

Association, I regularly read materials produced by those organizations and try to stay current with the schemes (and wrongs) of the Religious Right. I told the parent about these groups and referred her to online materials that explain the rights of students and the true meaning of religious liberty (I even mentioned the activism of The Satanic Temple with their emphasis on freedom for all beliefs, religious or otherwise).

Following her meeting with the principal, the parent called to relate the conversation. I was eager to hear about it. This is where the story gets more interesting, and instructive. You see, this parent is an assistant coach at the same school. She is also a Christian minister and pastor of a large Protestant church. Furthermore, her husband, also a Christian, is a coach and teacher in the same school. In other words, these parents have credentials and clout, with deep experience in the world of sports and faith. In this sit-down with the principal, the parent-minister spoke plainly: what's happening is wrong and needs to stop, it is coercive and exclusive. She wondered if other parents knew about this activity since, by all appearances, it was school-sponsored. There was no viable option for a player to choose to be apart from their team during practice time. She emphasized that as a clergyperson herself, she would never push her faith on these young athletes. She knows of at least one Jewish athlete on the team, and there ought to be respect for any other religious beliefs or atheists among the students. The principal seemed to agree, then called in the athletic director who listened to the parent's concerns and complaints. The principal and director assured her they would address the problem.

One issue here is similar to what we see in other locations across the country when schools allow employees or outside sectarian representatives to provide "counseling," invite to services or conduct Bible readings or prayers. The kind of responses to challenges or push back on these activities include: "We've always done it this way," "No one's ever complained before" or a nonchalant, "Who cares?, it's just a prayer."

Why don't many students or athletes complain? Put yourself in their shoes, in their uniform, on the team. How would it feel to hear: "If you don't want to pray with us, you can stay in the locker room." Would this be a "pray to play" message? Should any student ever feel excluded in their own public school? As for the response, "We've always done it," that doesn't mean it's right, or legal. And this brings up all the appropriate Constitutional questions that need to be addressed along with ethical and educational questions.

If an administrator, or preacher, sees no problem with permitting one religious group or representative on school grounds among a captive audience of students, they should be educated about the separation of Religion and State. Absent a clear response to remedy the situation, AU, FFRF and others can send letters to the school or school board outlining the legalities including potential lawsuits. Some of those involved in these evangelistic efforts may have good intentions, yet, resistance to correcting this kind of problem may arise from a mixture of arrogance, ignorance and "God is on my side" self-righteousness. The preacher may become quite defensive, asserting his own "rights." However, doing the right thing, especially in the context of public education, gets priority over even the best of intentions.

Overall, I'm encouraged by the pro-active intervention exhibited by this parent-clergy-coach. As I see it, the way this was handled and addressed could be a model for other communities. It shows the value of communication and relationships between people of faith and secular humanists.

We are waiting to see sincere, substantial, significant results.

23
**Cherry-Picking Christians
& Tomato-Throwing Atheists**

As a freethinking humanist who is not anti-religious, I sometimes face challenges from aggressive atheists. Oddly enough, I often find myself defending religion, people of faith, and specifically Christians. This comes from many years as a liberal Christian minister serving as an interfaith chaplain. I don't abide those who pride themselves in being mean-spirited, who seem to have nothing better to do than wage attacks (and cheap shots) on battlefields in their minds.

In one online post I spoke out against White Christian Nationalism (WCN), something I see as a great threat to our secular democratic society (I'm a staunch defender of freedom of religion, the rational and Constitutional protection of diverse beliefs). I'm deeply concerned by those who seek to inject their sectarian beliefs into our public institutions and laws while asserting the nation was founded as their own godly government. I'm thankful to Goodness, as many are thankful to God, there is a historic guiding principle of separation of religion and state which protects anyone with faith or without. I will stand up and speak out for anyone's right to believe whatever they believe, as long as it doesn't infringe on anyone else's beliefs. My main concern is holding the "wall of separation" established by our unique secular Constitution.

One response to my post was from someone who identifies as an atheist. They were in agreement with me about WCN, but went on to criticize all Christians. "Christianity itself, without "nationalism", does pretty much all of this, especially the version that Paul invented. One has to cherry pick it to get anything decent out of it." In response I wrote: "Yes, however, a great many Christians who are not WCN practice more of an ethical kind of faith based on the more earthly, humanistic teachings of Jesus rather than the superiority of the Pauline Christ. There's always some cherry-picking with these things, or we could call it discernment, wisdom, freethought. . ." Then this reply: "Yep, that is true. Christians make up their god in their own image and pick and choose their way through the bible. It's not discernment, wisdom or freethought. it is making something up you like."

There was one more round to this round robin. I replied, somewhat tongue in cheek: "You're right, some do cherry-pick, just as some atheists tomato-pick. I think it comes down to our experience with Christians. Some cherries, and some tomatoes, are actually good." This obviously upset the apple-cart. The commenter shot back: "Funny how atheists only agree that there are no god or gods. So do tell how we "tomato pick" with one idea???"

While deciding if this "discussion" was going anywhere other than a minefield, I clicked over to this person's website. It was easy to discern the basis of their attitude and attack posture. They define themselves as someone who takes pleasure in the humiliation of others. I wouldn't normally try to engage them.

I've experienced this kind of antagonistic atheism even among some former clergy who are angry with their former fellowship and can't accept anything positive about religion, especially Christianity. When I've suggested this is due to a lack of experience with varieties of religions and religious people, it stirs a firestorm of emotion. Though I affirm that many people have been deeply wounded by their personal experience with faith, and I share some of the reasonable doubt that causes a person to make a rational decision to leave faith, it often seems the case that people paint all religion or all Christianity with the same bristly brush. My fairly positive experience with the liberal church and interfaith work over the years formed a different and I think more balanced perspective.

Perhaps against my better judgment, I replied once more to the commenter: "I mean, tomato-picking some Christians and some rotten fruits out of one massive, diverse religion then throwing tomatoes at all Christians. Like atheists, Christians don't agree on many things as well (even what a Christian is). Generalizing about a religion and then tomato-picking this and that concerning how they interpret their scriptures or how god is viewed is what I'm talking about. There are many discerning, wise and freethinking Christians. This may not be your experience, but there are many. Instead of picking and throwing cherries and tomatoes, why don't we show White Christian Nationalists, as well as other religious people and atheists, there is an alternative to the hate and bigotry? It doesn't have to be a messy battleground."

If we're looking for it, it's easy to see the rotten fruit or vegetable in the basket or bunch. We can choose to pluck out the bad and throw it in anger, or enjoy the gardens and orchards, and share the good harvest.

24
Seneca, Wisdom & Living Well with Nature

Born about the same time as Jesus of Nazareth, Lucius Seneca was a Roman writer, administrator and Stoic philosopher. Stoicism emerged from the teachings of the Greek thinker Zeno 300 years before Seneca's time, and takes its name from public lectures and discussions on the *stoa*, or porch, in the Athens public square. As scholar Robin Campbell writes in his Introduction to "Seneca: Letters from a Stoic": "The Stoics saw the world as a single great community in which all men are brothers, ruled by a supreme providence..." This divinity could be called "divine reason, creative reason, nature, the spirit or purpose of the universe, destiny, a personal god ... even, 'the gods'." Living in harmony with this universal force was central to Stoic wisdom and ethics.

Seneca's letters reflect his desire to pass along any wisdom he has gained as a Roman official who is also contemplative. Similar to the *Meditations* of later Stoic Emperor Marcus Aurelius, there are many thoughts in Seneca ripe for contemplation and serious pursuit of wisdom (philosophy). In Campbell's view, Seneca's commitment to philosophical excellence "was grounded on a belief that her end was the practical one of curing souls, of bringing peace and order to the feverish minds of men pursuing the wrong aims in life." One of the first true essayists in history, Seneca felt: "What we say should be of use, not just entertaining." Whether spoken or written, words carry influence and impact our daily lives, at least they should.

To get a sense of his Stoic views, a flavor of his wisdom, here's a brief selection (and good Roman numeral practice):

"It is not the man who has too little who is poor, but the one who hankers after more." (Letter II)
"You ask what is the proper limit to a person's wealth? First, having what is essential, and second, having what is enough." (Letter II)
"The first thing philosophy promises us is the feeling of fellowship, of belonging to mankind and being members of a community ..." (Letter III)
"Our motto, as everyone knows, is to live in

conformity with nature." (Letter III)

And living well is something the gods didn't give and can't do for us; it is a practice and process:
"Who can doubt ... that life is the gift of the immortal gods, but that living well is the gift of philosophy? (Letter XC)

The universal principle of reciprocity, or "do unto others," appears in Stoic thought:
"If you wish to be loved, Love." (Letter IX)
"No one can lead a happy life if he thinks only of himself ... You should live for the other person if you wish to live for yourself." (Letter XLVIII)
"Never to wrong others takes one a long way towards peace of mind." (CV)
"I should find it difficult to say which [people] annoy me most, those who would have us know nothing or the ones who refuse even to leave us the small satisfaction of knowing that we know nothing." (Letter LXXXVIII)

A sense of resignation (fate, destiny, fortune) weaves through Stoic thought. Bad things happen—storms, ill health, floods and fire:
"These are conditions of our existence which we cannot change. What we can do is adopt a noble spirit, such a spirit as befits a good person, so that we may bear up bravely under all that fortune sends us and bring our wills into tune with nature's ..." (Letter CVII)

Stoics believed in keeping our mortality in mind every

day in order to live more consciously and ethically:
"Death ought to be right there before the eyes of the young just as much as the old." (Letter XII)
"One thing I know: all the works of mortal man lie under sentence of mortality; we live among things that are destined to perish." (Letter XCI)
"Death you'll think of as the worst of all bad things, though in fact there's nothing bad about it at all except the thing which comes before it—the fear of it." (Letter CIV)

Most schools of Philosophy or Religion tend to have a few rivalries with other teachings. One gets the impression Seneca doesn't care for that; he likes to play with his friend Lucilius who wonders why Seneca enjoys quoting the sayings of Epicurus:
"Why should you think of [these sayings] as belonging to Epicurus and not as common property?" (Letter VIII)
"Whatever is true is my property ... the things of greatest merit are common property." (Letter XII)
"Whatever is well said by anyone belongs to me." (Letter XVI)

Like any great teacher, Seneca expressed what he learned from life's lessons. "[People] can prove that their words are their own: let them put their preaching into practice." (Letter CVIII)

25
If Everyone Believed the Same as I Do

According to the Roman Stoic, Lucius Seneca, who lived at the time of Jesus, assisting someone to live their highest ideals is challenging. One needs to be a good student with a good teacher. When the educational relationship breaks down, Seneca says: "part of the blame lies on the teachers of philosophy, who today teach us how to argue instead of how to live." Another part of the problem is that students come to teachers "with a view to developing not their character but their intellect." When this happens, philosophy is transformed from the study of wisdom to "the study of words" (Letter 108).

This observation was on my mind when reflecting

on a thought about beliefs. I wondered: if everyone believed as I do, what would learning, or belief itself, look like? Though I've had frequent run-ins with the word "believe," and don't think of myself as a believer in anything, I could stretch the word a bit and describe my "beliefs" in the following ways:

-I believe that saying "I believe" essentially means "I think" or "in my opinion."
-I believe that believing is not the most important thing in life.
-I believe that human beings have a responsibility to be responsible creatures.
-I believe the natural world, the cosmos, is all there is, all we have.
-I believe that it is generally good to have many systems of belief, as long as they are healthy and do not harm other beliefs.
-I believe it is wise to question "unquestionable" beliefs.
-I believe that reason and the search for wisdom (philosophy) can be enhanced or hindered by beliefs.
-I believe in encouraging others to express and explain their beliefs, and I believe I will be asking questions drawn from the well of my own beliefs!

A critical caveat here: *these beliefs do not originate in religion or faith.* They are innate. It's true, my religious upbringing and years in ministry helped shape these beliefs. I acknowledge that. However, just as my mind did not simply drop into my head, so my beliefs, that is, my outlooks, perspectives and feelings about the world evolved naturally over time. Personal experience matters; how we interpret those experiences matters; and what we believe is ultimately beholden to our life experience. I believe in being honest about that.

Wisdom. I don't believe in wisdom, but I try to honor a commitment to its pursuit. Wisdom must decide and direct our beliefs. To do so, what we already believe cannot direct wisdom or the pursuit of it. This is why voices like Seneca's are so important. I don't have to agree with everything he says and I certainly don't "believe" in Seneca. His philosophy is instructive; it's lasted through the tests of time (as long as the teachings of Jesus). He speaks from his (First Century, Roman, Stoic, male, wealthy, powerful) worldview. Once that's established with any teacher—including any founder of a religion—we can perhaps find assistance for our search for a wiser life, eyes wide open.

We have to be careful here. Philosophers—instructors in the fine art of living wisely—don't usually stand up and say: "Follow me, live like I do." Christian history, with its central emphasis on Jesus as a divinity in a robe and sandals, has denied Jesus the role of philosopher. Any pragmatic instructions, any practical lecture notes he may have left, are forgotten, dismissed as irrelevant. He didn't teach ethics, he taught himself, they say. It's all about him—not Jesus on earth but the Christ in the heavens. That isn't philosophy, not the way to wisdom.

A wise teacher needs to present alternative perspectives, to give instruction for how to choose the wisest way of living. Did any of the disciples live like their teacher? We get hints, glimpses, of their ethical lives, yet mostly we hear of their faith—their beliefs. And they sought, through preaching and writing, to convince everyone to believe just as they did. Of course, this is the origin and foundation of the missionary endeavor, evangelism, the propagation of "our faith."

There was a period of time when I believed "sharing my faith" (convincing others to believe as I did) was everything. One reason for this, the context, was a firm belief instilled by evangelists that "the End was Near" and it was my responsibility to convert the world to my views. A fearfully sad prospect!

Seneca speaks of character, a Greek word meaning "mark" or "engrave." What is the engraving that distinguishes us and leaves a lasting mark on others? Is it our beliefs, or our living?

Would I want others to believe what I do, to think as I do. I don't believe so.

26
Sagan Saves Us from the Demon-Haunted World

I'm the first to admit I get weary and discouraged by so much anti-science and anti-reason nonsense. In our time we're swimming in those muddy and polluted waters. The river of irrationality floods the land. It's never far away. A relative recently wrote of the "so-called vaccines." This relative believes, based on their beliefs, abortion is the major moral and political issue. And, though they won't come out and say it, they believe I'm going to a very hot place when I die, accommodations provided by their "loving Father." Should we argue? Mostly we steer clear of contentious issues. I'm more convinced that the best reasonable people can do—and I mean both secular and religious thinkers—is to keep presenting the "gifts" of science and reason, continually lifting up the good things done in the name of freethought and humanism.

Of course we need to stand up firm against the tide of nonsense, superstition, and especially the power-hunger of Christian nationalism. But vast numbers of religious people aren't spending their days forcing their faith on others, or trying to legislate their morality. They aren't going to throw out their faith by force anyway. "Lead by example" or "teach by model" is something I learned in ministry. Why shouldn't seculars practice the same thing? Sure, present facts, hold to what we know or sense is true, then show there's a better way, present a more fulfilling, joyful, way of living. Humanistic ethics benefit everyone, faith or not. I choose to respect what's respectable, while trying to be respectable myself.

Speaking of respect, when I need a dose of clear thinking from a wise mind I often open a book by Carl Sagan. He brilliantly addressed the rough edges, battered walls and minefields between science and religion, reason and superstition. He reminds us to pass along the "good news" of the scientific method because it's a "candle in the dark." Sagan is honest and sensible. For him, science is imprecise, messy and sometimes frustrating but it's all we have to explore and understand our world. He encourages us to ask the hard questions, of religious beliefs and our own views. Perspective should always be open to adjustment; admitting we might be wrong is a step toward wisdom, an essential aspect of the pursuit of wisdom.

In his timeless later work, *The Demon-Haunted World*, Sagan touches the match to the wick: "[There's] so much in real science [as opposed to pseudo-science] that's equally exciting, more mysterious, a greater intellectual challenge—as well as being a lot closer to the truth." The scientific endeavor is a continual search for facts, truth, useful knowledge of our world, the cosmos. If we stumble over its mistakes, the blunders of that exploration, we can find stability in remembering that *methods matter more than conclusions*. "The method of science, as stodgy and grumpy as it may seem, is far more important than the findings of science." We don't have to look very far to see how so many get tripped up by the uncertainties of science—resistance to public health directives, defiance to mask and vaccine rules, and general distrust of both the findings and the process of science.

In one of his most cogent passages Sagan helps clear the muddy waters of arrogant ignorance: "Science is far from a perfect instrument of knowledge. It's just the best we have. . . Science invites us to let the facts in, even when they don't conform to our preconceptions." This conceptual framework leads straight to what Sagan calls "one of the great commandments of science": "Mistrust arguments from authority." This doesn't mean we don't listen to any authoritative, knowledgable sources, but we think for ourselves, follow the data, face the realities head on, not merely accepting someone else's opinions. Sagan goes on to point us back to nature: "In its encounter with Nature, science invariably elicits a sense of reverence and awe." This stirs a celebration of "the magnificence of the Cosmos."

With Sagan as a guide, we can wrestle with the shadowy parts of religious beliefs that so often stand as obstacles to human progress and critical thinking. Along with him we can shed light on the demonic superstitions that fly out of the dark caves of fearful faith.

As a youthful evangelical, I was taught to fear the demons, the "powers and principalities in heavenly places" as Paul imagined them. Faith was a constant battle against the fearful temptations and assaults of The Evil One and his sneaky minions. I saw people "possessed by spirits," and those "delivered from the power of satan" who was "cast out" by preachers who claimed those superhuman powers. We were constantly on guard to protect our fragile and fear-based faith from spiritual forces who apparently had nothing better to do than lead young minds astray.

With more years of enlightened thought and broader experience in the open air and sunlight, I was able to let go of these dark clouds of superstitious beliefs and feel truly delivered, released, liberated. When we're possessed by destructive beliefs, it takes great effort and resilience to break free.

Confronting the real demons of our world together

is essential. In my evangelical college Greek class I learned that a *daimon* is not something to fear, we all have a *daimon*. The hope was to have a *eu-daimon*, a good spirit or heart, in order to enjoy *eudaimonia*—happiness. So, for me, confronting our demons is a two-edged lightsaber. We stand firm as enlightened educators before the "powers of darkness" (irrational, ignorant systems) and we are presenters of the light, goodness, an ethical lifestance and reasonable skepticism. Darkness dies in the light.

Sagan states a matter-of-fact truth: When people believe that gods descend to earth, they see those gods coming down, when they believe in fairies or spirits or aliens, that's what they see. This is the power of belief, of credulity, accepting the words and worldviews, the myths and mysteries presented by forceful traditions and their zealous converts. As Sagan sees it, there are more wonders and beauties in nature than anything imagined in super-nature. With the eyes to see we are able to observe what the great astronomer noted, that there seem to be no religions that sufficiently honor "the grandeur, magnificence, subtlety and intricacy of the Universe revealed by science." I would also have to agree with him that scriptures can't hold a candle to modern science, they never spoke to the universe we are coming to know more and more through rational investigation. There is no technology or practical outlines for human culture. They offer little assistance in our quest not for other worlds but for the only one we have.

I was somewhat startled to read these lines from Carl Sagan's widow Ann Druyan describing the importance of publishing his lectures in 2006:

"In the midst of a worldwide pandemic of extreme fundamentalist violence and during a time in the United States when phony piety in public life reached a new low and the critical separation of church and state and public classroom were dangerously eroded, I felt that Carl's perspective on these questions was needed more than ever." (Acknowledgments, conclusion to *The Varieties of Scientific Experience*).

In 2006! How prescient she was, and was her husband, to address the pandemics of that time, as the echoes of ignorant beliefs ring louder and wider today. Even now we have to wield the sword of truth and slay the demons so that, in great relief we can sing together: "Ding, dong, the demons are dead!"

Hail Sagan!

27
Does Rising from the Dead Matter?

On Easter Sunday a column rose up to my attention in *The New York Times* proclaiming: "Why it matters that Jesus really did rise from the dead" ("What John Updike and Gerard Manley Hopkins knew about the power of Easter," Tish Harrison Warren, NYT, April 17, 2022). She begins with the proclamation: "Christ is risen." "He is risen indeed." She explains: "These words, with slight variations, will echo today in many different languages as most Christians around the world celebrate Easter. They are a statement of hope. And the church has always proclaimed that they are a statement of fact: that Jesus truly did rise from the dead. Christians mean these words literally." She goes on to quote from Updike about Jesus 'body, cells, thumbs and toes, etc.

Warren sides with Updike, who is, she argues: *"pushing back on an idea that became ascendant among mainline Protestant churches around the turn of the 20th century and still exists in some places: that belief in a bodily resurrection is incompatible with modern science, technology and medicine."* My brow was already furrowed—"still exists in some places"? Then she continues: *"But many who rejected the literal Resurrection of Jesus wanted to maintain some kind of Christian identity, so the story of Christ rising from the dead was recast as a purely spiritual event or a metaphor, not strictly, materially true. In contrast, Updike almost roars: "Let us not mock God with metaphor."* Well, roaring aside, I find it puzzling a priest like Warren pushes both a "spiritual event" and metaphor aside. One could say, and indeed many biblical scholars feel, that the Bible is full of many "spiritual events" and metaphors. I understand, she is reacting to making the resurrection a "purely" spiritual thing, but I would argue the whole story has a spiritual screen over it, so much so it's difficult to get a handle on something to put our hands on. This is not to say, and I'm not saying, there is no historical fact woven into these stories. Yet, the Easter story (let alone the Good Friday story) is so literally unbelievable we are left with the author's faith or a freethinker's skepticism.

The writer makes quite an astounding statement: "Whatever else Christianity is, it is an assertion of historic fact. The New Testament invites us to examine the evidence." I don't hear that invitation; mine never appeared in the mailbox through all my years of biblical study and ministry. No, Christianity is an assertion of faith and invites readers to believe without evidence. That would be more truthful.

As I wrote to some friends, I have so many issues with the views presented in the essay.

If one believes everything literally in the Bible, her view fits that worldview, but that's pretty hard to sustain. Of course, if you believe in every "miracle," the resurrection is one of many, and every one of them is based on faith, not evidence (many things are "unexplained" but that doesn't mean they are miracles). That there was no body matters, but not in the way we were taught in Campus Crusade—fact is, we have no body of Moses, Buddha, Confucius, Muhammad, or even Paul for that matter. Were they all resurrected? The columnist asserts, with Paul, that without a bodily resurrection there would be no faith. This seems extreme, as Paul's letters often are. My question would be: So, none of Jesus' teachings about love, justice, compassion, forgiveness--basic ethical principles--are worth living, or dying, for? That seems to neglect and disrespect the life and teachings of Jesus. We might wonder why he didn't simply drop from the sky onto the cross and then fly back up.

Warren is troubled by the age-old line from Christian apologists (defenders of the faith): If Jesus didn't walk out of the tomb in the flesh, why would so many of his followers die for a "lie"? Like so many tried-and-untrue quips from apologists, this is similar to the false dichotomy that Jesus was either the Lord or a Liar. Serious biblical scholarship offers more options than these extremes suggest. Early Christians lived and believed and often died because they thought the story was true. They trusted the storytellers, those who relayed their own experience and beliefs about their divine teacher. It wouldn't have been a "lie" to them since only a few people said they saw Jesus after death. They chose to believe what others told them (Thomas Paine called this "hearsay, not revelation"). And so the full story of Christianity, and the entire history of religion, is based on traditions-- handed down beliefs.

One further response. The whole argument that early Christians gave their lives for a "lie" completely ignores the fact that Jews, Muslims, Buddhists, Pagans, Indigenous Peoples, Humanists and others have died for their faith or commitment, and continue to do so. Once again, a Christian-centric telling of stories, any stories, always gets it wrong since it isn't considering the wider context. Then, if it's a Conservative or Evangelical-centered narrative, even more skepticism is called for.

It's clear where the writer places herself in the story, because in her view believers are part of the story— they participate in the resurrection, somehow. She says: "the only real evidence that that is any more than wishful thinking is rooted in history, as solid as a stone rolled away. The Resurrection happening in truth, in real time, is the only evidence that that love in fact outlasts the grave, that what is broken can be mended, and that death and pain do not have the final word." In other words, if you aren't a Christian, or aren't a Christian who believes like she does in the literal, historical, "solid" resurrection story, there's nothing to show you that love endures or that pain isn't the last word in our lives. A rather audacious if not arrogant claim. The faithful priest apparently has no knowledge of other narratives, of the Hebrew Bible, the Bhagavad Gita, the Qur'an or other scriptures, or even secular sources that don't view death as the final word in the human story. No, for her, it's an Easter Body or nothing.

Warren agrees with Updike that relating these ancient stories as metaphor somehow "mocks God." You'd think good conscientious writers would not mock metaphors. A metaphor is simply a transfer of meaning, a figure of speech that makes something non-literal sound literal. An open-minded, liberal Christian (of which there are many), still finds great meaning in a resurrection metaphor. It's not that "it didn't really happen," because that's no longer the point. The point is a compassionate life and meaningful death. the exclamation point for a life of ethical action and teaching. Metaphors can be powerful motivators to "resurrect" the best in us, faith or not.

Tish Harrison Warren concludes that Easter "if it's worth anything at all, is more than a metaphor. But it is more than mere history as well. It happened in a specific hour 2,000 years ago yet it cannot be captured in time. It is earthy and palpable but also a sign and a symbol pointing to a reality more mysterious than I can name. The Resurrection spoke the unsayable."

"More than a metaphor"? "Mere history"? "Specific hour"? "Earthy," and pointing beyond, to some other reality? Odd what faith can do to mere reasoning sometimes. In my mind, that last phrase fairly sums up the entire essay: The whole strange sacred traditional tale of a dead deity coming back to life, a body walking out of a tomb, is ultimately "unsayable." It has not been seen and cannot be said. Oh well, another mystery, another miracle, another reason to dismiss the metaphors and those who may sincerely believe and attempt to walk in the earthy footprints of the dead Jesus who became, by the faith of the faithful, the living Christ.

When it comes to religious faith, does rising from the dead matter? For some, yes, for others, no. This is precisely when a freethinking humanist happily steps in to referee, saying: Imagine if he did not come out of the tomb. How would a life committed to the good, loving and just be different? If the resuscitation of bones, blood and brain was important to the faith of some disciples and Paul, that doesn't make it a lie, just their error. If you believe in a living God, ok. If you believe Jesus literally, bodily, rose from the dead, ok. But how do we live together here, now, this side of death, Body believer, Metaphor believer and nonbeliever? Isn't that what honestly, truly, matters?

28
When Flora & Fauna are Friends

My friend Heather has been a nurse practitioner for years. I first met her when she founded a critically-needed medical clinic at a downtown agency serving many of the same people I worked with. Nurses, social workers, therapists, chaplains can make a good team when the concerns are the same—the health of human beings. Years later, after earning her doctorate, Heather became a professor instructing nursing students. With longterm dedication to caring for the health of others, she also has the heart of compassion for the health of non-human living things. As a master gardener, she tends her plants, birds, insects, slithering and scurrying things that inhabit the land they share, and she does this with a tender thoughtfulness. She's like a nurse for outdoor things.

I've always admired the way Heather refers to so many living things as "friends." "Well, hello, friend!" she might say to a newly opened flower, vegetable sprout or neighbor cat. "Oh, you look thirsty" or "Don't you look happy today!" It comes natural to her to address Nature and all living things in a personal, and respectful way. I've learned to do this myself. It's fairly natural for me to speak to another being, to honor the fact that we have at least one thing in common: sharing life on a spinning rock in space.

"Well, aren't you beautiful!," I may say to a bobcat or bear. "What are You?" I may ask the insect, bird or spider I've never seen before. If a critter is in a bad place—say, a corner of the bedroom, I may say aloud: "You have to go outside," as I capture it and put it out with a "There ya go!" My wife Carol appreciates spiders, at least the smaller kind, and she knows various arachnids are healthy for the environment. But when it comes to the larger variety—and we see some doozies here in the South—I'll hear Carol's voice calling to me and I know it's going to be another capture and release.

One spring evening she told me with a shudder there was a large spider on the wall outside the garage. "Good," I said, causing mild irritation. Later in the evening I heard that tell-tale voice calling out. Somehow the spider made it into the garage and was approaching the kitchen door. Pointing to the intruder with a gasp, she left the eight-legged roundup to me. Trusty glass and notecard in hand, I had little trouble nabbing the—good sized—critter and brought it in. Carol stepped back and held the door as I dropped the interloper off the deck into the bushes—"There you go, out where you belong," I whispered. Mission accomplished. My assurances that she could do that herself were not assuring to Carol. I'm not exactly thrilled by *big little things* either, but I don't mind these gentle interactions.

Heather has always been a cat-lover (I'm not) and likes having more than one around (I wouldn't). Whenever one of her felines would catch a bird and triumphantly drop it at the door or at her feet, Heather would feel bad for the bird and gently scold the cat. She knew the cat was simply doing what predators do, but it hurt her to see a dead bird. I think she was troubled to hear me read her a report one time that cats kill millions of birds every year. I guess some "friends" are a little more valued than others. I don't mind a few cats now and then, but I prefer the flying friends.

Talking to flora is different, at least in my mind. Heather will talk to flowers and vegetables. I might whisper to a tree, especially the old rugged variety, but what we have in common is a sense that it matters. As I see it, we know these living things don't "hear" our voices and certainly don't understand language, yet the act of speaking to them reminds us humans that we're related, interconnected, with all rooted, branching, blossoming things. Surely with food plants we should be constantly conscious of our dependence and interdependence. This isn't some new-age woo-woo or even tree-hugging, though I've embraced a few conifers.

Without flora and fauna, human life is empty, and, well, dead. And so would be much of the meaning and joy.

I suppose the whole point with these furry, feathery or flowering friendships is how much they matter to us, how deeply we think about the relationships and what we think friendship really means. Heather and I have grown apart, in part because I got married and moved across the country. I suspect we will always be connected though, rooted in the same earth, delighting in our natural environments, and enjoying many of the same friendships that feed the body and the mind.

These reflections drew me back to something Jane Goodall wrote in *Reason for Hope*: "[My years studying animals] had not only helped us to better understand their place in nature but also helped us to understand a little better some aspects of our own human behavior, our own place in the natural world."

Maybe if we saw our own reflection in the eyes of our natural neighbors we would enjoy the companionship of many more friends.

29
1619 & Beyond

I've been reading *The 1619 Project*. I'm aware of the controversy about the NYT project, and noted that the authors had made several corrections, so I wanted to read it for myself. Based on what history I've read, I find *The 1619 Project* an enlightening historical analysis. It makes sense and should be taken seriously.

On the wall behind me, as I sit at my writing desk, is a copy of the Declaration of Independence (seems appropriate for freethinkers to have one on display; and, by the way, it's not called the "Declaration of Independence," it's "The Unanimous Declaration of the Thirteen United States of America"). Be that as it may, the copy bears the signatures of 56 white ... male

...landholders.

There seems to be strong evidence that reveals a majority of our Founders, the "Sons of Liberty," were slaveowners. While owning other human beings, they could sign a document that claimed "All men are created equal" and their rights include "Life, Liberty and the pursuit of Happiness."

We can honor and respect these people for their revolutionary actions. . .while at the same time we can, and must, "hold these truths to be self-evident". . .that they were far from perfect, they had major blind spots and they were personally involved in dehumanizing other human beings including Native Americans, African-Americans and their own wives.

Of the American Founders, 34 were slaveholders:
Josiah Bartlett, Charles Carroll, Samuel Chase, Abraham Clark, George Clinton, John Dickinson, William Floyd, Benjamin Franklin, John Hancock, Benjamin Harrison, Joseph Hewes, Thomas Heyward Jr., William Hooper, Stephen Hopkins, Francis Hopkinson, Thomas Jefferson, Richard Henry Lee.
Francis Lewis, Philip Livingston, Robert R. Livingston, Thomas Lynch, Arthur Middleton, Lewis Morris, Robert Morris, William Paca, George Read, Benjamin Rush, Edward Rutledge, Richard Stockton, William Whipple, Thomas Willing, John Witherspoon, Oliver Wolcott and George Wythe.

The ones who apparently did not own slaves (yet surely

had colleagues, friends or family who did):
John Adams, Samuel Adams, George Clymer, William Ellery, Elbridge Gerry, Samuel Huntington, Thomas McKean, Robert Treat Paine, Roger Sherman, Charles Thomson, George Walton, William Williams and James Willson.

"Princeton University history professor Sean Wilentz noted that at least four men in the [famous Constitution Hall] painting, including Franklin, were or later became abolitionists. Also, in 1776, slavery was legal in all 13 of the new states and was "condoned by the entire West," including Britain and France, he said. 'As the men who drafted and signed the Declaration were mostly gentlemen of standing and property, it's not at all surprising that this would be the case,' Wilentz added. (*The Chicago Sun-Times* and *Politifact*)

As Nikole Hannah-Jones writes in her essay on "Democracy":
"[One] of the primary reasons some of the colonists decided to declare their independence from Britain was because they wanted to protect the institution of slavery." True, not "all" but "some," yet the fact remains: defending "liberty" in many minds meant defending "slavery."

"White sons of Virginia initiated the drafting of the Declaration of Independence, the Constitution, and the Bill of Rights. The primary authors were all enslavers. For the first fifty years of our nation,

Southerners served as president for all but twelve years ..."

To be a truly freethinking, educated American, I think it's essential we face the racism inherent in the founding of this country, and open our eyes to address the continuing effects of white supremacy. If some find that troubling, it's an American kind of trouble that agitates for change. With all the uproar about being "woke," maybe we need a good dose of reality, the shock of awakening.

Lastly, for white folks who may want to challenge these historical viewpoints, I would ask:
-Have you read *The 1619 Project*? (can you dismiss these historians? how?)
-Perhaps more importantly, have you read Frederick Douglass, Sojourner Truth, Harriet Jacobs, Harriet Tubman, or listened to other Black voices including W.E.B. Du Bois, Zora Neale Hurston, Langston Hughes, James Baldwin, Martin Luther King, Jr, Audre Lorde, etc.?
-Are you aware of what happened in Reconstruction, or during Jim Crow, or the segregationist decades that led to the Civil Rights movement and legislation?
-And, if you're serious about this, have you asked your Black friends or colleagues what they think and feel about this more honest and accurate view of American History?

Whole History, or History with Holes?

As a teacher concerned with streams of thought,

particularly Freethought, I'm continually asking myself who is being left out in the stories we tell, whose voices are not being heard. Though I'm no historian, I'm aware that pulling one thread of the historical narratives is only one thread. To teach history accurately is to teach history honesty.

Listening to Ezra Klein's interview with Nikole Hannah-Jones and Ta-Nehisi Coates, who both teach at Howard University, these images and ideas came to mind:

♦ History is like a knot, or better, a twisted thread made of a variety of multi-colored strands

♦ People have a reaction when one strand is touched, pulled or emphasized (think: BLM, Women's Rights, other sexualities, etc). American history is usually taught as primarily one thick *white* thread or rope. Some get agitated when another color is held up. Btw, this is not simply about race

♦ If we teach healthy skepticism, we will hear from people and voices who are not the "authorities" with their "official reports"

♦ History has to be seen through more than the Lens of Power (interpreted by the dominant)

♦ History, like biography, needs to show both the good and the bad of individuals and institutions

♦ There is anger and pushback when the White (or male, or Christian) thread is not given the most privileged place in the narrative

♦ We are not responsible for what our ancestors did, but we are responsible for telling the whole story truthfully, and for what we do with that now

We either do our best at teaching Whole History (accurate, truthful, balanced) or we end up teaching History with Holes (with important threads missing).

When I teach, I always make it clear I am not a historian; I am choosing to highlight several threads bound together. The twisted cord is long and open for exploration ... many strands, many cords!

Further thought for consideration: people, and communities, are woven threads too. Are we hearing, and telling, the whole story?

30
Build a Bridge, then Get Over It

Here in the American South, we see many kinds of signs, symbols, stickers and flags. It's not unusual to see a Confederate flag on a truck or flying on a porch or along the highway. It's also true in this truly diverse land to see a variety of mottos and slogans, some political, others religious, or simply thoughtful or humorous.

Now and then we put an American flag in the window on election day or simply to show we "Libs" are Americans too (I sometimes quip that if I'm called a "Lib" I guess I can call a conservative person a "Con"?). Anyway, we all like to "fly our flag" once in a while, to say what we're for or against, to make a statement, though that statement may not be the original intent of the banner (wasn't the flag of the United States about being "united" not divided?).

Strolling through our local Farmers' Market, I walked by a kiosk with handmade wood plaques painted with different expressions. As we often see in markets and stores, these signs are sold to hang in an entryway, a living room, office or den. The one that particularly caught my eye that day said: "Build a Bridge, Then Get Over It." I didn't purchase it, but carried it in my mind driving home. Since I regularly speak of my writing and teaching as "bridge-building," especially between people of faith and freethinkers, the humor of the wooden plaque seems to "nail it" when it comes to the meaning or purpose of bridges.

First, it is our responsibility to build. No one else can do that. However, building a bridge alongside someone else may be the only sensible way to construct one.

Second, the bridge isn't something we build just for others because we think they should cross.

And *third*, "getting over it" suggests we have some work to do beyond the building project! This may be calling attention to the fact sometimes we can't seem to let go and get going. Besides, some spans may not be prepared to carry heavy loads of whatever we cling to.

Carol and I sometimes playfully banter after one says:

"Get over it," with the response: "Get under it," then "Get around it." You get the point. This keeps things light, though there may be a more serious reason for the initial nudge to let something go, to move on. It's easy to get stuck on one's side of things, on an opinion or judgment. Another person jabs us with a "Get over it!" The wooden sign goes the next step, literally. In essence: "Drop your attitude, view, or stuckness; leave it on that side of judgment, build a way across to a better attitude." Something like that.

Come to think of it, the plaque I saw at the market would have been perfect for my chaplaincy office, my shelter director work as well as the door of my manager's office in the senior housing work. Bridges of communication, cooperation and some form of community, were essential foundations, requiring daily practice. Never easy.

And let's imagine the sign hung up in a prominent location on the doors to congregations and sanctuaries. What do religious believers need to let go of? What if those stuck on beliefs could get over Theology or an addictive obsession with ancient scriptures? Or, more basic, how could those places, and those within, become spaces and faces that invite crossing to wider connections across the "dogmatic divides"?

Of course, as with many phrases or quotes like this, probably the best place to hang it up is in our head. It could be a helpful reminder to tack these kinds of enlightening motivational truths on the doorways of our consciousness.

31
From the Moon to Making Meaning

I was reading about an astronaut who was one of the last to walk on the moon 50 years ago (WaPo, April 22, 2022). He described the amazing experience, his wonder looking up at the earth. He gathered dusty stones to carry back, rocks that geologists say could be over 4 billion years old. A half-century later, this astronaut now believes the earth and the universe are only 6000 years old and God made it all in six days. When it comes to Science, he'd rather believe the Bible, as he interprets it. Quite an orbit.

In a column on how we endure suffering, loss and grief, NYT columnist David Brooks addresses the psychic disruption that occurs during turbulent periods in life. Experiencing life's traumas we have to find ways of "regaining control over [our] beliefs. The mind is a relentless meaning-making machine." He says following great losses we sometimes create mental blame, fears and unhealthy ways of handling our pain. Then Brooks offers this insight: "At moments like these, we don't always have thoughts. Our thoughts are having us" ("Some People Turn Suffering Into Wisdom," NYT, April 21, 2022).

As my mind works, I quickly connected these two readings. An astronaut has incredible experiences walking on the moon, returns to earth and starts a business; facing struggles in his family, he attends an "intensive Bible study" with his wife and becomes a born-again Christian. Now, he trusts his scriptures more than anything he used to know from years of education and training. People cope with loss and fearfulness by allowing thoughts to seize and save them.

We usually think of people having beliefs. What happens if we turn that around and upside down? What if our beliefs actually have us? We choose to believe some things and those beliefs guide us for good, or possess us. Those beliefs take over, our bodies, our minds, our whole outlook on the world, on our lives, past, present and future. Everything else, including what we've learned from parents, teachers, experience, fades or becomes less important. For many, it seems, committed believing takes precedence over critical reasoning. Bible trumps textbook; spirituality trumps science; faith trumps freethought; religion trumps reason.

Worldviews can be earthviews or moonviews or otherworld-views. Which world are we in and how do we make sense of it? Beliefs can take us to other worlds, far off heavens and the abode of the gods. When our dreams and hopes grab ahold of a myth that promises to take us away from terra firma, it can be a powerful gravitational pull. Good old mother earth is left behind.

Even the Bible presents various worldviews, a diversity of perspectives, with a deity who creates worlds, and destroys them, who desires wisdom yet demands belief. When back on earth, the astronaut read Genesis and chose to believe that a six day creation erased evolution. In other words, he became a literalist. As I see it, when a book, any book or scripture, takes the place of serious thinking or devalues human relationships, it can become *literally* destructive, dangerous. If this astronaut had been more faith-directed than fact-directed before blasting off for the moon, would he have gone at all? Would it all have simply been a spiritual journey looking for God in the heavenly places? Would he have shrugged off the whole mission as a futile human attempt to understand the cosmos instead of trusting the Cosmic Creator? In other words, would the mission have been his personal mission of faith, not for scientific knowledge but to know his God better?

Now he travels around sharing his good news story of a "young earth," a 6000-year youngster of a world doomed to end up desolate as the moon if the planet doesn't become fundamentalist Christian.

Walking on another world, like the moon, must be incredibly wonderful. Like all explorers, astronauts show great courage as well as an almost childlike exuberance in the delight of discovery. Religious faith can sometimes enhance those moments, filling an adventurer with gratitude. Or, those religious feelings can overwhelm, causing a person to revert to a childlike dependence on heavenly arms and ancient books (as I read the astronaut's account, it came to me that his choice to be "born again" was a choice to become a child again, to jettison all he had learned in mature years for a childlike faith).

I understand our need for a "meaning-making machine." If that machine is functioning properly we may receive some wise direction in decision-making. Yet, if it's lost in space or stuck in spaciness, it may one day fall back to earth. That could be a hard landing.

32
The Benefit of a Basement Perspective

From my basement office I loudly whispered up the stairs to Carol: "There goes our bobcat!" Slowly walking by the ground-level window to the left of my desk, the gray huntress rounded the corner to amble by windows in front of me. Slipping upstairs, I joined Carol in the bedroom to gaze down, watching in wonder as the wild feline sniffed plants and insouciantly sauntered on.

When you spend a good deal of time on the "ground floor," you notice many things that go unseen by those above, "up there." For me, it's essential to look out into the trees, down the valley, continually aware of changes in weather, of light, clouds and wind, and wild things closer to earth.

At various times in my life I lived in basements. During depressing transition periods I endured the dark and damp of downstairs rooms or low-rent apartments. In one case, an empathetic Catholic couple opened a tiny room in their basement for a temporary shelter. Another time, an Episcopal priest and his wife allowed me to sleep in a lower part of their home while I struggled to find adequate housing. A young seminary couple gave me a space on a lower-level office floor where my young daughter and I slept for a short while. Though it wasn't a basement, one other period of precarious housing brought me to a room in the far end of a Presbyterian widow's home. While scrambling for a place to lay my head during a relationship breakup, I slept in a tent in a state park for a few weeks before moving into the home of a New Agey lady—in her basement, of course, when that got flooded out, I moved my meager belongings up the street to another tiny room. I guess you could say my basement experience has been ecumenical.

Ironically, or appropriately, I endured some of these experiences while serving as a chaplain among unsheltered people! I was counseling "housing challenged" individuals and families from a knowledgable position. The few who knew of my uncertain "home life" showed great concern and compassion. Clearly I was "experienced" in the search for home. I certainly know what it feels like to have "temporary housing."

Now, my office/den/man-cave is below, downstairs. Though it can be the coldest spot in the house, slanting rays of sun find their way in at certain times of the year. I watch the season's change here, lower down, closer to the earth. When the squirrels scurry by, nuts inflating their cheeks, I know winter is coming. When rabbits bound passed, turkeys strut by, and twilight brings the silent steps of the bobcat, spring has arrived, and I sense it's not long before the big furry neighbors—black bears—plod by. The heat of summer has arrived when I catch a glimpse of a black snake slithering along or ascending a tree.

Of course, through all these passages of time, singing is sure to be ringing in the air. The constant ebb and flow of the bird-tides, the endless fluttery flit of winged neighbors is delightfully distracting. My computer screen has its back to one set of windows, so even with the onset of cataracts, my peripheral vision catches any movement out the glass. I'm ready at a moment's notice, to notice, to slowly get up from my chair and move quietly to a window for a closer view. Is it an insect I've never seen, a chipmunk, or something larger? Do I pick up my camera or just observe? What's happening on the ground, nearby, under those trees, in that flower bed, across the patio? What's Nature doing right here, right now? What can I learn in this moment?

A basement can be a descent to a new level of

awareness. You can see the animals and birds at their level, eye to eye. You know you can walk out and be on solid ground with them, and all other terrestrial creatures, into the sun and rain and open air. I sense I'm in a living, moving classroom where the teachers are full of surprises and tricks to play with my attention. Lessons abound down near the ground.

Establishing a baseline. Having a basis for your views. Running the bases, or making it to home plate, home-base. Many ways to consider and reflect on the basics, of the day, the environment, of life. I admit I enjoy a very comfortable basement now, in the present time. I say it this way since I vividly remember all those earlier periods when a basement wasn't just an office or den but a shelter, a roof, a short-term haven for a weary guy.

My baser instincts tell me a basement is foundational, in a literal as well as life-affirming way. Down here I can go up into my head, do some creative thinking, or wander out, where the world is full of deeper lessons and higher things to contemplate.

33
Henry Thoreau's Woodsy Meditations

It's been twenty years since my little collection of wisdom from the Walden wanderer was printed. *Meditations of Henry David Thoreau: A Light in the Woods* was published in 2002. It came second in the series that began with *Meditations of John Muir: Nature's Temple* (2001) and continued with Emerson, Whitman, Fuller and Burroughs. Muir has been the most popular but Henry holds his own (most copies of the later books have been gifts). He is always sauntering nearby, since he first gave me that descriptive word, *saunter*, picked up by the ever-sauntering John Muir.

The book was dedicated to my father and his three brothers who all served in WWII. I also honored

"Companions who hike the higher lands and climb the trees." This was a verbal hug to some close friends who've shared those hikes and climbed with me into the swaying branches of trees primarily in California. If you're familiar with the books in this series you know that each selection from the natural philosopher is paired with a brief quote from another thinker. So there are sixty selections from Henry and sixty companion quotations—from Gandhi and Buddha, Confucius and Jesus, the Qur'an, Bible and Upanishads, Mary Oliver, Barry Lopez, Coleridge, Eliot, Whitman, and many others. It brought great satisfaction to place so many great thinkers alongside the Walden Wanderer, the Forest Philosopher.

The collection opens with this short "meditation":

"The indescribable innocence and beneficence of Nature —of sun and wind and rain, of summer and winter—such health, such cheer, they afford forever!" Then the joy overflows: *"Shall I not have intelligence with the earth? Am I not partly leaves and vegetable mould myself?"* Here he speaks of "great-grandmother Nature" and the intoxicating morning air he imagines bottling to sell. Henry's enthusiasm is contagious.

In another chapter, on the "Comforts of Life," Henry identifies the true characteristics of a philosopher: *"To be a philosopher is not merely to have subtle thoughts, nor even to found a school, but so to love wisdom as to live according to its dictates, a life of simplicity, independence, magnanimity and trust."*

Those passages are snipped from *Walden*, but there are powerfully insightful passages from other works such as *A Week on the Concord and Merrimack Rivers*: *"[The] most excellent speech finally falls into Silence. Silence is audible to all men at all times, and in all places."* One clear example of Thoreau's playful use of opposites and puzzles (something that apparently irked his friend Emerson). From *The Maine Woods*, one selection draws from Henry's earthy language when he describes drinking in the wild wonders in the North: *"as if we sucked at the very teat's of Nature's pine-clad bosom."* One who imbibes all the botanical flavors of the woods would "see green" and dream of the wind in the pines. In the chapter on "Springs of Life," from his essay "Walking," we hear the meditative saunterer remind us that walking is not so much for bodily exercise as it is an opportunity to ruminate "in search of the springs of life." And, from "Wild Fruits," Thoreau offers us a taste of life's goodness and health: *"Live in each season as it passes; breathe the air, drink the drink, taste the fruit ... Nature is but another name for health."*

About ten years ago I took a quick walk around Walden Pond. I didn't have much time, but it was a memorable, emotional circumambulation. Before leaving I stepped into the shop there and spoke with the manager. He was pleased to meet me and made sure to display copies of Thoreau, and my other books. It's always brought me contentment whenever I see my books in National Parks or other bookstores around the country, or when someone tells me they've seen my books in parks. This was the whole intent of my writing projects from the beginning—to spread the "good message" of wise thinkers who go to the Great Classroom of Nature, I suppose because I'd like to be "naturally wise" too.

In the summer of 2020, early in the pandemic, I taught an online course entitled "Ripples from Henry's Pond: Thoreau's Freethought Voice." Many were engaged with the man especially in the unorthodox context of freethinking. Students responded with many exclamations: "Enlightening" and "Warm, inviting, exciting." "Another fascinating and stimulating class!" "Fabulous instructor. Having taught American Literature for 20+ years, I thought I was well-versed in the subject. To my delight, [the teacher] presented new ways of looking at the material that had never occurred to me!. The class was delightful!" As for the "fabulous instructor," I think that should first and foremost refer to Henry himself.

I won't try to shamelessly sell the book in this book, though I will mention that *Meditations of Henry David Thoreau* has sold over 16,000 copies and will be in its third printing this year. The real reason I bring up the book at all is this:

We may need to "meditate" with Henry more than ever.

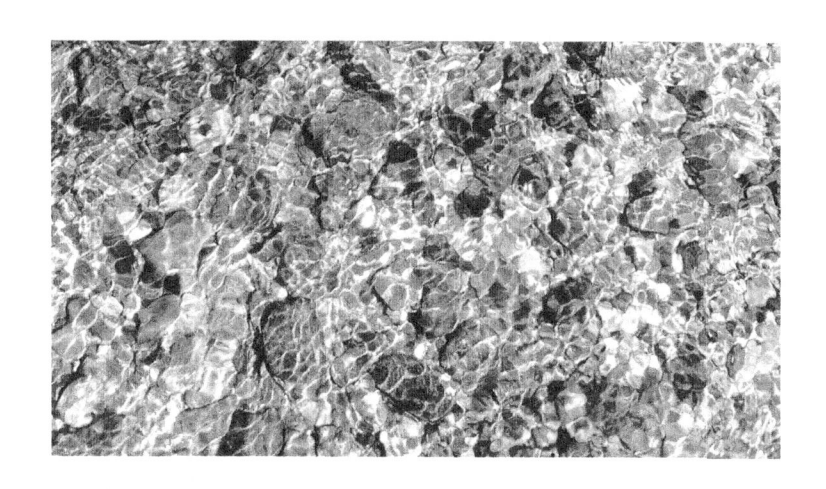

34
**The Nones Bible, Chapter One:
Is There a Religion of Love?**

> *I posted this seven-part series on*
> Friendly Freethinker *in 2020*

You've heard of them. When asked to name their religion they respond, "None." They don't identify with any particular religious faith. They may claim to be "spiritual" or to believe in some form of "god," but they won't let us pin a label on them and say, "Aha, you're one of them!" And, maybe that's a good thing.

Well, today we begin a series I'm calling: *The Nones Bible*.

These are brief essays that take a hard look at

traditional "sacred" stories and teachings from a non-traditional, freethinking point of view. If you're one of the Nones, you may not know there's a "bible" for you (well, there is, and it's being written now). If you're an agnostic, atheist, skeptic, freethinker, you may not realize there's a "bible" for you too (well, there is, and it's the natural scripture of life *minus* the supernatural).

Hopefully, no matter your beliefs or non-beliefs, you're sufficiently confused now, which means you're ready for the first chapter of...*The Nones Bible*

Chapter One: Is There a Religion of Love?

As a child, our Sunday School class learned to sing, "Praise Him, Praise Him, all you little children, God is Love, God is Love." I think there were hand motions as we sang in front of the congregation causing smiles and nods of approval from our parents and the pastor. We were so cute, you know.

As a teen, I helped out during my home church's vacation bible camp and led children in the same song. "God is Love, God is Love!"

Thinking back on this, with a slight cringe, causes me to wonder what would have happened, to me and all the other little children, if that song had told the whole story of faith, if those lyrics had been the central message of the church. In other words, what if there really was a "Religion of Love"?

The other verses in that song we were taught as

children were "serve Him," and "love Him." "God is love" meant "loving God." A subtle but significant twist.

My question now is: If there actually was a Religion of Love, would you or I be followers? What would that religion look like? And might that transform if not revolutionize the world of faith?

These are not simple or simplistic questions.

In my youthful days as an evangelical, we memorized verses and sometimes put them to music. One song was based on First John 4:7-8: "Beloved, let us love one another; for love is from God, and the one who loves is born of God and knows God" (I still write this from memory). Then we read, "Whoever does not love does not know God, for God is love."

What if it stopped there? Not just the scripture passage—the whole religion, the entire faith? What if this encapsulated the "good news" of the Love Religion?

Surely some will hasten to say, "Wait a minute! Our religion teaches love. Our God calls us to love. Our scriptures and our religious teachers show us how to love. Our faith is truly a 'religion of love'."

Yes, I hear that and understand. But this is not what I'm suggesting.

Subsequent verses in First John reveal exactly what love means and how to prove a person is a true believer. "In this is love, not that we loved God, but that he loved us and sent his Son. Since God loved us, we ought to love one another." Next comes the remarkable line: "No one has ever seen God; if we love one another God lives in us ... ." Then we hear it repeated, "God is love." (4:10-12)

These passages in early Christian writings show us that loving is about believing—love is proof of faith. Yet, that love must be generated by a belief in Jesus as God. Otherwise, no love is possible.

Or take these famous lines from the Gospel of John (13:34-35): "I give you a new commandment, that you love one another. Just as I have loved you, you also should love one another. By this everyone will know that you are my disciples, if you have love for one another."

So, this is not a true religion of love. It's a religion of Jesus. You must believe in Jesus to love, and you must love Jesus to believe. You cannot "merely love" others —authentic love is found in only one faith.

And, who can be "commanded" to love?!

The faith-love unity isn't restricted to Christianism of course. At the end of the great revelation chapter in the Hindu *Bhagavad Gita*, Lord Krishna speaks to the bedazzled Arjuna: "Only by love can people see me, and know me, and come unto me. The one who works for me, who loves me [and has] love for all creation, that one in truth comes unto me." (11:54-55)

Here again, love is faith-bound, specific to one faith, one god.

A true religion of love would be a practice of lovingkindness, not a system of beliefs. It would not require theological assent, creeds, dogmas. It would not require scriptures at all. There would be no manual or privileged class to instruct us in what love is or how to practice it. Otherwise, we would have to wonder if it was "love" at all.

A religion of love would not require membership, only commitment to do what love requires. What is that? We would need to work it out, think about it, try and fail and try more.

A religion of love would probably be no religion at all.

Has there ever been a true religion of love? If so, where? when? How did that work and what happened to it?

There are moments in time when we see evidence of this, but the question is whether it's a "religion" or simply a "practice of love" itself?

Mohandas Gandhi and Martin Luther King, Jr. remain among the best representatives of this ideal (and perhaps Dorothy Day and Dolores Huerta). Gandhi wrote that religion will not survive if it doesn't understand that "God is Light, not darkness. God is Love, not hate. God is Truth, not untruth" ("Young India," 1924). In his 1957 speech on "The Power of

Nonviolence," King said: "I am quite aware of the fact that there are persons who believe firmly in nonviolence who do not believe in a personal God, but I think every person who believes in nonviolent resistance believes somehow that the universe in some form is on the side of justice."

These voices offer us a "middle way" between faith and atheism—an invitation to "take a side," to join the religion (or philosophy, or daily practice) of truth, justice, enlightenment ... and love.

35
**The Nones Bible, Chapter Two:
Who Really Believes the Bible?**

This may sound unbelievable and I can't believe I'm saying this, but there are times when I wish we could find some folks *who really believed the Bible*. I suppose I should explain.

First of all, when I say "believe the Bible" I don't mean what many seem to mean when they say they believe it. I get the feeling that there are huge numbers of people who believe they believe but they really mean that they believe this or that part of the book. It's natural and human to be picky and choosy. But it would be nice if these folks would honestly admit they're selective, avoiding uncomfortable verses or stories.

Take the story of the "Rich Ruler" in the Gospel of Luke (18:18). He calls Jesus the "Good Teacher" and says he has lived by the Ten Commandments his whole life (consider all the Ten Commandments monuments going up around the country). But how does the "Good Teacher" respond? My paraphrase: "[Good for you, and nice shoes; now] sell all you own and give to the poor."

Stop for a second and think of all those "successful" people you know in your life. Have any followed this teaching ... ever? We all know that's crazy, right? No one in their right mind would give up what they own and give it away to poor folk, wouldn't you think? Well, maybe a "saint" like Francis of Assisi. But, it's plain nuts to actually DO this, agreed?

What's the explanatory defense we hear from "biblical scholars"? "Oh, this is another example of how Jesus uses extreme teachings to make his point —like the call for disciples to "hate father and mother" and follow him. He wasn't saying WE should literally do this—heaven's no! There's a 'deeper 'more 'spiritual' meaning."

So they say.

Let's not even touch the line, "But I say to you that listen, Love your enemies, do good to those who hate you" and a few breaths later, "Give to everyone who begs from you" (Luke 6:27, 30). What if someone, anyone, actually listened, and at least acted as if they believed it?

Maybe what we "believe" doesn't really matter—it's what we do, and that "believing"—especially believing a book—is often the greatest stumbling block to living up to the "real message." Something to think about.

We might also point to the inconvenient passages where Jesus suggests (?) that God has a particular concern for vulnerable people and despised outcasts. What do the "bible dancers" (interpreters) come up with? More contortions, distortions and locomotions. We can see them twist and shout.

I was thinking about my dear departed Dad. A good-hearted man, generous and devout, he "believed the Bible" and read it regularly, but I rarely heard him quote it, and he never read it aloud or preached from it. No, he lived it. How did he do that? He tried to live in peace with neighbors, always helped strangers and never stopped giving of his time and resources to the family, church, friends and others. Was he perfect? Of course not. But who cares? He lived, loved and listened for the meaning of the words he read and heard from the pulpit.

I have friends, colleagues and family members who "believe the Bible," though as I see it, they choose to believe the more believable parts, especially when it comes to compassion, justice and doing the right and good things (all taught by many other sources beyond the Bible, of course).

Now, does anyone understand why a former "Bible believer" can have deep respect for some who believe—and who live their beliefs with love and compassion?

Some will insist they truly "believe the Bible." It's not entirely sarcastic to ask, "Which page, paragraph or point?" When they answer that "It's ALL God's Word" then it would be natural to inquire, "Then why don't we see people obeying ALL of it?" At this point we often hear folks say they believe all of the book but there is an "Old" part and a "New" part and the "New" part contains "Red Letter" parts (and they have their favorite verses) that are truly, especially "God's Word." Sigh.

I have my red-letter, leather-bound Bible right here on my desk while I write this column. I could put my hand on it and swear an oath on it (which it says we should never do), but you would say I don't believe it, so you wouldn't believe me.

Alright. But could we agree to treat one another decently, fairly, justly, compassionately, with or without a book?

36
**The Nones Bible, Chapter Three:
Boys, Bears, Bald Prophets & Biblical Ethics**

Many speak of "family values" and "biblical ethics" while ignoring (conveniently overlooking or "creatively interpreting") some rather disturbing passages.

Like sticker-shock, the cost of some stories can be a little too high ...

As a "Bible-believer" for many years, I not only read the book cover to cover but studied, memorized and preached the book as God's Word. This one book was the highest authority for life, with everything I needed to know for living a "godly" and moral life. I wanted the whole world to be in the *divine book club* with me.

It was almost as if God had spoken every word necessary for the human race thousands of years ago (in Hebrew, on one tiny patch of earth) and then took a vow of silence. IF God ever spoke again, He would simply quote Himself. There was nothing particularly new to say.

When I began to dig deeper into the scriptures with a critical and open mind, taking the book in its historical, literary, psychological context, uncomfortable things began to appear. Those who taught me the Bible, respected teachers I trusted, somehow overlooked passages and verses that were the most perplexing. When they did talk about troubling parts or contradictions in The Word, they sometimes offered less than satisfactory explanations or interpretations. Maybe they didn't know any more than I did about these things?

Take a guess.

I was asked recently to read something in the Second Book of Kings concerning the dramatic life of the prophet Elijah. You may remember the famous story of Elijah's hiding on mount Horeb when the Lord "passed by" but isn't in the wind, earthquake or fire. The prophet hears a *voice in the silence* instructing him to hike down and keep moving. He has a mission.

The first order of business for Elijah is to get a disciple and the one he finds plowing with oxen in a field is

Elisha. Elisha drops the plow, kills and cooks the hard-working oxen, and follows his new master.

These stories may be familiar since they are favorites for preachers who like lessons of faith and miracles.

But ... I've never heard a preacher talk about the most shocking part of the story of Elijah on Mount Carmel: the prophet of the Lord personally executed 450 (possibly 850) non-Israelite prophets. So he proved his God was the "true god" and the others failed. He won. That could have been the end. He grabs a sword and cuts down every faith leader who challenged him.

Am I missing a "moral lesson"?

With that pleasant thought in mind, let's skip ahead to a "miracle" story that—miraculously—I've never heard *any* teacher or preacher ever talk about let alone attempt to explain.

Let's call it the "Holy Bear" story.

This little gem is found in Second Kings chapter 2 and comes just after Elijah catches his flaming chariot into the sky, dropping his clothes—ok, his cloak— which is picked up by his disciple Elisha. The new prophet uses the magic mantle to part a stream just as Moses parted the Red Sea.

Listen for the divine word:

"Elisha went up from there to Bethel; and while he was going up on the way, some small boys came out of the city and jeered at him, saying, 'Go away, baldhead! Go away, baldhead!'

I consulted one respected bible commentary on this passage. No comment. The sound of sheer silence.

Allow me to speculate. A novice prophet appears holding the cloak of his hero who has literally gone up in a puff of smoke. He's feeling pretty good, energized. Like a superhero, he has double the power of his mentor (he asked for that extra strength in the beginning of the chapter). He's just performed some nice tricks— parting the waters of a stream and purifying a town's water supply by pouring salt in a spring. His confidence is growing with these magical powers as he walks from town to town. You can imagine he was wearing Elijah's mantle like a superhero cape, maybe pretending he could fly.

Then a group of boys ruins it all. They gather around him, taunting, making fun of him. "Unacceptable!," he thinks, "I'm a Man of God! A prophet of the Lord of the Universe!" The mischievous kids don't throw stones or water balloons or try to grab his power-cape. No, they throw an insult. They dare to make fun of his hair, or lack of it.

"Baldhead, baldhead!," they laugh.

What does God's prophet do? Does he turn to the name-callers and teach them a lesson about compassion and kindness? Does he preach a message of hospitality and respect for strangers? No. He curses them in the name of his God, bringing about his third miracle: two mother bears charge out of the forest and kill the boys—*all forty-two little children torn to bloody shreds.*

Elijah kills hundreds of clergy; Elisha kills a bunch of name-calling kids.

The lesson of these stories? Maybe the Bible is not always the best source for ethics.

Note: perhaps the current frenzy of book-bannings have overlooked one of the most disturbing and dangerous books?

37
**The Nones Bible, Chapter Four:
Some Confusion About Where Believers Go
When They Die**

I don't make it a habit of reading obituaries. Like the old joke, I'm afraid I might come across my own death notice. But I sometimes read articles about people who have died and find it curious when people of faith speak of where their loved one has gone and what they're doing in the afterlife.

It's important to be careful when considering these delicate emotional times and the deep feelings of grief people are experiencing when they express their beliefs.

With that sensitivity in mind, I was reading the words

of one person who recently lost his father. He said, "My father has joined my mother in heaven. He went to sleep in his home ... and woke up in the arms of Jesus. While many around the world mourn his physical death, he is now celebrating the eternal life [he told others about]."

These words were spoken by someone who says they know the Bible very well. In fact, they "believe in the Bible." The Bible is the Word of God, infallible, to this family. We can respect that. We can also expect they would be consistent about what they believe, especially when it concerns serious issues such as death.

As I read the words of that grieving son, I remembered my own years studying scriptures. Recalling a passage we used to read in our evangelical group, I was puzzled. The words and the images the son spoke didn't seem to fit with a passage from Paul's First Letter to the Thessalonians, chapter four. The apostle writes about believers who have died, "so that you may not grieve."

"We who are left until the coming of the Lord (Paul believed he would see Jesus return) will by no means precede those who have died. For the Lord himself, with a cry of command, with the archangel's call and with the sound of God's trumpet, will descend from heaven, and the dead in Christ will rise first. Then we who are alive, who are left, will be caught up in the clouds together with them to meet the Lord in the air; and so we will be with the Lord forever. Therefore encourage one another with these words."

That's a lot to unpack. Yet, those who "believe the Bible" would have to handle some difficult questions.

How could Paul, the inspired writer of scripture, have been so wrong about being alive for the return of Christ? Was it fair to teach that to early believers? If "the dead rise first," then aren't they in the ground until that day? So, no one is "with God" or "in the arms of Jesus" until then, right? If living believers fly up into the clouds with the dead, how does Jesus "catch them" and where do they go?

It may sound sarcastic but we also have to ask: Does God really play a trumpet?

The mourning son wrote, "Today, [my father] is experiencing what he devoted a lifetime to telling others they could experience if they placed their trust in Jesus Christ."

Today? A believer goes directly into heaven and the embrace of God? This is odd. I thought we were taught since childhood that people "sleep" until the Day of Resurrection when the dead shall be raised.

Yet, this man's departed father once said, "Do I fear death? No. I look forward to death, with great anticipation. I am looking forward to seeing God face to face. And that could happen any day." Clearly he believed the moment he died he would see God. But what about Paul and his letter of encouragement to the believers in Thessalonica?

Why do we seem to get so confused about death? Maybe because it's Death, and death is a mystery that we desperately want to understand, to explain, to be comforted over.

Paul wanted to assure the early believers in the crucified rabbi of Nazareth that they would soon hear trumpets, see their dead friends and family rise from their graves, and fly up with them into the sky where Jesus swoops down to pick them up to soar beyond the clouds. It's very dramatic and leaves our thoughts floating in air.

I have grieved many times, and sat with people who are grieving. I learned to minimize words. Nothing to explain. Being with another in their sorrow is enough.

Assuring someone their loved one is in the Lord's arms, face to face with God, may sound like encouragement. I understand the powerful emotions that image provides. Though I don't see how that's better than being present, and silent.

No one knows if and when the dead will rise, but Death raises some trumpeting questions, does it not?

Note: I've been reading Anthony Pinn's book, *Writing God's Obituary*. An interesting story of his emergence from Methodist ministry to Humanist teaching at Rice University.

38
**The Nones Bible, Chapter Five:
Does Religion (Specifically Christianism)
Have an Image Problem?**

(Or, Does the Worship of Jesus break a few Commandments?)

I was responding to a reader who challenged my views on women's voices left out of sacred scriptures (by the way, I welcome the constructive comments and challenges), and was reminded of something that has troubled me for many a year.

Those who worship an ancient Palestinian Jewish rabbi as God have to do a little explaining when it comes to images. Catholic and Orthodox Christians have decorated cathedrals and churches with images of "The Lord" for centuries. Countless Protestant churches do the same. How many of us grew up with the face of Christ everywhere from Sunday School coloring books to stained glass windows to gold-framed portraits at church and at home (even in some public schools)?

Yet, I wonder, what if this deep need to "see God"—to stare into the face of Someone who is worshipped, and even pray to that face—is not at all what was originally intended by the God of Israel or Jesus himself? What if the proliferation of images is actually a violation of several direct commands?

Before anyone grabs their Bible to proof-text me, picking and choosing verses and worn-out theological arguments, let's be calm and clear: take a deep breath and keep in mind that I'm not "attacking" anyone's faith, merely raising some reasonable questions.

I know this is touchy, but a closer look at *The Big Ten* (not football this time) may be an interesting mirror for people of faith to consider (The Ten appear in Exodus 20 and Deuteronomy 5).

"You shall have no other gods before (besides) me."

The very first commandment tells us a couple of things. YHVH (LORD-Yahweh) recognizes there ARE other gods, and the Lord is concerned people may choose a different one.

Then comes something uncomfortable for image-makers: "You shall not make for yourself an idol (image to worship), whether in the form of anything that is in heaven above, or that is on the earth beneath, or that is in the water under the earth. You shall not bow down to them or worship them; for I the LORD your God am a jealous God."

The next command has to do with not "misusing the name" of the Lord. Is this perhaps warning us not to call God any other name but LORD (the unspeakable, unpronounceable "I Am" appearing to Moses on the mountain)?

If you want to talk about the Lord of the Universe ... you can't ... it's impossible as well as blasphemous.

Over my childhood bed hung a picture of a long-haired white man with folded hands looking up into the clouds. I was told this was Jesus and assured this was God. Now, no one, not my parents or Sunday teachers or preachers ever said this was the "real" Jesus or the "actual" God. "He" was much bigger than a picture. Yet, I would look around my world of faith and see many other representations of what the Jesus-God looked like. If you're like me, these images get imprinted, one could say they have been "engraved" on our brains.

Think of Jesus right now. Who do you see in your mind? Is that God? You may say, "Well, of course not, that's just a picture." But if that isn't what Jesus or God looks like, why do we imagine God looks like that? It's all we've been given, all we've been told represents

God. White, male, long hair, beard, clean ... in human form.

How does this image-problem become so pervasive?

We face a Face, but is it The Face?

If not, what's going on? Why create an image of the imageless?

In some strict Christian sects images are not allowed. Nothing to distract from "true worship" that recognizes no pictures or forms of the divine. Yet, again, what do people *imagine* is the image-less image of their God? (e.g., must have eyes and ears to see the faithful and hear their prayers).

Judaism itself never allows representations of the divine or uses the too-holy-for-words Name. Islam is very strict about this too. Images are not only forbidden, they are considered blasphemous. Allah (God) and the Prophet (Muhammad) are never to be visualized. This would limit and in a sense cheapen the whole concept of the Lord of the Universe. Like drawing a picture of a galaxy, a nebula or the universe itself.

After Moses received The Big Ten, the text says the Lord spoke "out of the fire, the cloud, and the thick darkness." The mountain-climbing prophet "heard the voice out of the darkness ... out of the fire."

Is this what people have overlooked for centuries? Some of the "saints and mystics" seem to have understood it, but most forget: voices from the darkness or whispered in fire can't be drawn or painted or sculpted ... or worshipped.

We may still wonder how Jesus would feel about the worship of his ubiquitous image. He disappeared into the dark cloud of history, while millions continue to make forms of "things in heaven and earth."

Doesn't it make you wonder?

39
**The Nones Bible, Chapter Six:
Eyes on the Clouds**

Observing incoming clouds this morning, blown along by a strong wind, I found myself reflecting on the fact those swirling wisps of vapor had probably been tornadoes not far away last night. Beautiful here, they wreaked destruction there. Soft, floating clouds of white, gray and black passing over the Blue Ridge destroyed homes in nearby states, lives were lost.

Several people who live in those areas said "Thank God!" it wasn't their house, their life. Another said that, since it was Easter Sunday, "we will rise together." Where does this belief come from?

There seems to be a lot of cloudy thinking in our world

today. And much of it can be traced straight back to old teachings from old texts in an old book—the Bible.

A refresher for those who've studied the Bible (and new "revelation" for those who haven't): Paul, in his first letter to the Thessalonians, gives specific details about where Jesus went when he ascended and how believers will ascend when The Ascender descends, again. Somehow, someway, this writer of most Christian scriptures, had some higher-insider information on the "other world," death and the mysterious movements of God—the divine ups and downs.

(This parallels the discussion of death in chapter 37)

"We who are alive, who are left until the coming of the Lord, will by no means precede those who have died. For the Lord himself ... will descend from heaven, and the dead in Christ will rise first. Then we who are alive, who are left, will be caught up in the clouds together with them to meet the Lord in the air ... ." (4:15-17).

Let's try to get the picture: After walking out of the grave on Easter, Jesus flew into the sky; someday very soon, he will soar back down to escort his believers up; dead Christians will float up first; then Paul and his band of believers will float up into the clouds to meet Jesus; the whole assembly will fly off to heaven to be with the Lord for eternity. A very dramatic scene.

Paul writes these things because he doesn't want the Thessalonians to grieve their dead or lose hope. So, he tells them this fantastic story to assure them they will soon be flying up with him. "I'll fly away, O glory!"

As a young Evangelical, these words of assurance were on my mind every day. We cried through Christian films, concerts and endless sermons that promised: "Watch the Clouds! He's Coming Soon!" Everyone was overwhelmed with expectancy that Jesus was returning, not only in our lifetimes, but very soon. We were ready!

This is the so-called "Rapture"—the snatching up into the sky. What we never thought about in those heaven-minded days was that Paul believed he personally would be alive to see it. Jesus himself believed this cloud reunion would be happening right away, to those who heard his voice.

The fact that it didn't happen as Jesus and Paul believed it would, seemed to have no effect on our youthful expectations or the propagation of the Gospel of Clouds. Jesus was gone, Paul was gone, and generations, even centuries, of Christians believed "He's Coming Soon—in our lifetimes!"

Yet, the clouds pass over and move on. "Angel's hair" for some, while they "block the sun" for others, clouds "rain and snow on everyone" (Joni Mitchell, "Both Sides Now").

In Paul's "sky story," he doesn't want the congregation to be "uninformed" about death, about what was yet to come. Today, we might question how Paul got that information and whether the people were truly informed about life and death (Saul, aka, Paul, claimed to vacation once in the "third heaven"—he didn't want to "boast" about it, of course, but he was "caught up into paradise," where he "heard things not to be told" ... you know—see Second Corinthians 12).

Voices, visions, flights of fancy. All a little cloudy, aren't they?

A freethinker approaches this atmospheric story with great skepticism, of course, yet also with some disappointment and sadness. For thousands of years people have pinned their hope on the clouds, looking up expectantly. They have believed the Lord is coming back, descending so they might ascend as he did into the clouds. I remember the emotion: "He's coming for me!" Yet, even as Paul was about to have his head removed by a Roman blade, he must have had a concerned look on his face, glancing up: "This would be a good time to take me up, Lord!"
And we remember the promise of Jesus to the thief crucified near him: "*Today* you shall be with me in paradise."

As a chaplain for many a year, it pains me to hear such promises. According to the Gospels, Jesus did not go to paradise when he died that day. It was long afterward that he "ascended into the clouds." They might sound comforting, or draw more converts, but these airy promises can actually be quite cruel.

Keep your eyes on the clouds. Think of what they

bring to people all across the land, across the earth. Tomorrow, there'll be other clouds. Who knows what they'll bring?

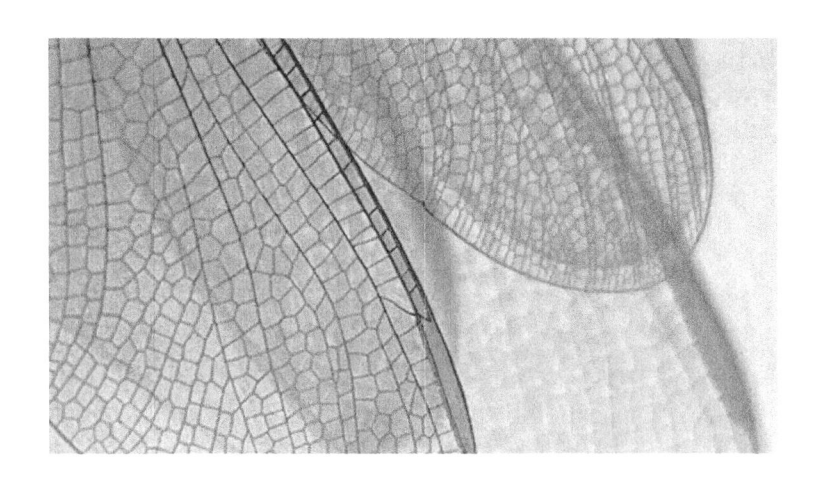

40
**The Nones Bible, Chapter Seven:
A Mantle of Protection for Beliefs**

There are biblical stories of protective cloaks, robes or mantles that may be familiar to many readers (Elijah, Ruth, Jesus). One commentary describes these garments as "wrap around" clothing often worn by wanderers, strangers and the poor. A mantle was protective covering even used for sleeping (which makes me think of the Scottish kilt).

In our time, we may compare capes, shawls or serapes—even cozy blankets or rain ponchos. There's something very comforting about being surrounded with protective covering to shield us from the cold or heat, wet or wind.

This image of the mantle got me thinking about great thinkers who considered protections for all of us when it comes to our beliefs or non beliefs. This may sound like "just politics" but it seems to me to be "just freedom"—a central teaching of all religions as well as secular philosophies.

Visiting Thomas Jefferson's home at Monticello we were impressed by the architecture, the land and the gravesite. Of course, we were also saddened as we imagined all the slaves tending the grounds, gardens and household. It stuns the senses and common sense to think such a great mind, devoted to freedom, could be so blind to his own human property.

Jefferson's gravestone is carved with the two accomplishments he was the most proud of: "Author of the Declaration of Independence" and of the "Statute of Virginia for Religious Freedom." When he and fellow president John Adams both died on July 4, 1826 they were remembered for revolutionary acts as well as some fairly revolutionary ideas.

One of the most influential ideas the Founders left in the documents they handed on to us was the idea that in America citizens were free to choose whatever religious beliefs they desired, or choose no religious beliefs at all. Quite a radical concept.

Near the end of his life, Jefferson commented on those who wanted to craft "religious freedom" laws to primarily protect one faith, their faith:

"The bill for establishing religious freedom, the principles of which had, to a certain degree, been enacted before, I had drawn in all the latitude of reason & right ... its protection of opinion was meant to be universal. Where the preamble declares that coercion is a departure from the plan of the holy author of our religion, an amendment was proposed, by inserting the word 'Jesus Christ,' so that it should read 'departure from the plan of Jesus Christ, the holy author of our religion' the insertion was rejected by a great majority, in proof that they meant to comprehend, within the mantle of its protection, the Jew and the Gentile, the Christian and [Muslim], the [Hindu], and infidel of every denomination." (Autobiography Draft Fragment, July 27, 1821).

Imagine what America would look like if that amendment had passed! When one religion attempts to assert its supremacy, "reason and right" must step in to correct and balance. As Jefferson saw it (ultimately joined by the rest of those who decided America would be different than other nations ruled by one faith), the "mantle of protection" would be "universal" and included a variety of faiths as well as "infidels"—freethinkers with unorthodox opinions.

At Monticello I took photos of the house, as everyone does. I also captured images of a beautiful yellow and black spider in its garden web, a stick bug in a bush and a bright blue butterfly (we travel for nature as well as history). Then I saw one tree with interlaced roots protruding through the grass. That image seemed the best one to illustrate what I was feeling on that historic ground: this is *our ground* (Monticello, Virginia, America), all of us, with faith and without faith, any party or none. Like the threads of a well-worn cloak or mantle, synapses in our brains, or the veins in our skin, we are held together, rooted to freedom—the tree stands and shelters.

Does this sound like politics or religion? Isn't it really about *people*, the human community? The mantle is for all of us, even when we don't want "those people" under the same spreading tree or mantle of protection.

Though it might be fun, we don't need an "invisibility cloak" as in Harry Potter, or any magic at all. Jefferson's mantle is a "wrap around" to make everyone visible, not invisible. The Founders' philosophy was concerned with protecting the rights, the freedom of conscience, of each person by acknowledging the differences and letting them be. There would be plenty of disagreement and debate under this mantle, but that doesn't have to rip us apart, it can make the threads and roots stronger.

And what about those "infidels"? Jefferson himself was accused of being one though he called himself a Christian at times—as well as a Deist and Unitarian. The best guardians of the mantle may be those infidels—not beholden to any one sect.

It's good to know the mantle is owned by no one ... and everyone.

41
When Things Don't Add Up
(or, Like Knife Through Butter)

I find an interesting parallel in Carl Sagan's *science* education to my own *religious* education. In his preface to *The Demon-Haunted World*, he writes respectfully of honored professors who "not only understood science, but who were actually able to explain it." As a physics student at the University of Chicago, he was grateful to find a learning environment "where science was presented as an integral part of the gorgeous tapestry of human knowledge." A study of the Classics, History, Art, Music, Psychology and other disciplines presented him with a broader context to understand the integration of science with all human explorations.

Under the mentorship of his professor of planetary astronomy, G.P. Kuiper, he came to appreciate a major guiding principle of science: If your theories and calculations don't add up, if you don't find that your answers are the best explanations for a problem, "you look for a different explanation." Sagan discovered this simple rule-of-thumb-and-thinking "cut through nonsense like a knife through butter."

The most influential and inspiring teachers in my own educational journey handed me sharp knives as well. The more I studied Religion the more butter I found! Yet these teachers, in college and seminary, presented me with that wider context so significant to Sagan. A more open landscape of experience and thought made it possible for me to consider alternative perspectives that offered a deeper appreciation for the good in religious practice and beliefs. Butter was one ingredient in various recipes for a workable worldviews. But did those life recipes really work? Were they practical, healthy or half-baked? Uncovering those ingredients, whether nonsensical or sensible, was an essential step in revealing any lasting value in particular religious views.

The thread I followed through my formal education was wisdom, the pursuit of wisdom I first encountered in Philosophy. Something clicked, a light came on, from Philosophy 101 onward. Some of my pious professors were committed to useful knowledge. They understood religion and could explain difficult religious concepts. As Sagan said of science, religion was presented "as an integral part of the gorgeous tapestry of human knowledge." Wisely, they nudged me to a series of "tentative conclusions," taking a stance that affirmed: ideas are powerful fires for the intellect and burn bright across a continuum of possible conclusions. Harness the fire of ideas and ride them wherever they take you. A basic foundation was laid: with more open books come more open minds.

Was my course, my pursuit of wisdom, my fiery ride with ideas, going to lead me to a clearer path of faith or to a wiser philosophical road? Though I had the desire to remain at Seattle Pacific to teach and seek more intense study, I chose to explore the possibilities in ordained ministry. With some regret, but with both a professional and personal curiosity, I left my native Washington for California where I could apply what I'd learned and build on that. I would gradually realize —with many tentative conclusions in the process— that the wise way of life was to serve people who lived with a lot of butter to cut through. I soon learned that I wasn't the only one with knives. Incisive discernment, and wisdom itself, appears in most unexpected times and places (I tell more stories of ministry and chaplaincy elsewhere).

Another close corollary to Sagan's education and my own is expressed at the conclusion of his preface. He states that he learned "the most essential things not from my school teachers [or] university professors, but from my parents." They didn't have knowledge of science yet their early encouragement of skepticism and wonder, their evident valuing of education, gave him the freedom to explore, question and accept the gift of science.

I could say similar things about my parents, Robert and Mabel. They were people with a quiet yet abiding faith, who took me to Sunday School from childhood, though it was their support for my religious exploration and experimentation with faith experience (seeing me through evangelical, pentecostal, "messianic" and philosophical stages) and their complete support of my college and seminary education, that truly inspired. They set me on the path, though they had no formal religious education. They trusted I would find a way, my way, and loved me through every step.

Mom and Dad have been gone many years now, and, as Carl Sagan greatly missed his parents, I still miss mine very much. Their grounding influence continues. Even as a freethinking secular person I will always honor their example of simple decency, quiet faith and "education through life experience" that gave them practical knowledge and technical skill (Mom in office administration and Dad building planes at Boeing). And when my thoughts, ideas and beliefs don't add up, I always have a few knives at hand—along with melting humor mixed with common sense—left to me by my parents, prepared to cut through

CHRIS HIGHLAND

the nonsense.

42
Primitive, Childlike, Yet the Most Precious Thing

Astronomer and hero of skeptics Carl Sagan opens his book on *The Demon-Haunted World* with this quote from Albert Einstein: "All our science, measured against reality, is primitive and childlike—and yet it is the most precious thing we have." I imagine this would be a fine response to any flippant dismissal of science or any of the anti-science nonsense we hear so much today. Primitive refers to what is prime, primary, original, perhaps undeveloped, like a theory, conjecture, new idea. Childlike seems an apropos description of any honest and open endeavor to learn. To do good science "ye must be born again," we might say. Be ready and willing at any point in the search for knowledge and truth to begin again, to see things with new eyes, new experiments—a renewed commitment to go forward with the insatiable curiosity that drives the best of science, philosophy or religion.

Why would science be precious let alone "the most precious" thing? Sagan leaps right into our contemporary dilemma, the tension between science and pseudoscience. He argues it may be hard for some to accept reasonable, scientific explanations for their cherished miracles and mysteries. In biology and archaeology, chemistry and astronomy, every investigation into our world and our cosmos offers wonders even the most spectacular supernatural tales can't hold a candle to. Fake science can lull credulous people into believing just about anything, yet it is intelligent science that "arouses a soaring sense of wonder." Fear or dazzlement at the *unknown* causes the old God of the Gaps thinking. Sagan cites the ancient Greek physician Hippocrates: "Men think epilepsy divine, merely because they do not understand it. But if they called everything divine which they do not understand, why, there would be no end of divine things."

I passed along this quotation recently during an email exchange with a believing friend who was criticizing physicists for probing into the unknown. When everything become divine, or "spiritual," we are prone to see our gods everywhere. My friend spoke of God's "omnis" (omnipotent, omnipresent, omniscient). His god is Christian, a very specific strand of Christian, so his *omni* is Jesus. In his view, if a scientist doesn't understand something on the long and incessant search for knowledge, he or she simply hasn't found the hidden Christ yet. My friend and I used to be in the same evangelical culture where all roads lead to Christ, at least our beliefs about him. He was "The Answer" to anything and everything. This is the beginning and end to the age-old conflict between Science and Religion. If you already know what (or who) you will discover here, there and everywhere, that no theory really matters, that it's not about the pursuit of wisdom but God, then there really is no use for science (or critical thinking) at all.

No wonder science is the most precious thing. And a treasure not only for discoveries, but the search, and the pure delight—though hard work—of every search.

A good example of this sense of delight can be found in a favorite passage from Charles Darwin's *Voyage of the Beagle* in 1836. In South America, he takes long walks, "glad to find my enjoyment of tropical scenery." As he saunters, he notes that the diversity he sees and hears and touches proves the "exquisite natural beauty" of nature's simplicity. He observes "the wild luxuriance of nature" in the "brilliant sun of midday." It's a "hopeless endeavor" to describe or paint the scene. He tries to put a pen on page to sketch what he sees, yet though he "wishes to find language to express" it all, words are "found too weak" to express "the sensation of delight." This is a man overwhelmed by natural wonders as his curious nature leads him deeper into the forest.

Enjoyment, beauty, quiet admiring, sensation of delight, gazing upon beauties, glories, one perfect scene, beauty, beauty. Are these the words of a scientist? Maybe not in the popular mind, or in strict religious thinking, or by some laboratory researchers, but these are indeed the words of a naturalist exuberantly stumbling over language, knowing he must say something that honors what he has never seen, and few may ever see. He has a "mission" to explore, to study, to investigate and carry back questions for other searchers—he must write in order to remember, and to bring others along in their imagination, joining the adventure, the exploration that is living science, though the words are wholly inadequate.

Darwin ends this passage while in San Salvador, awed by all he sees, yet aware the land and forests would remain but the beauty would fade, "like a tale heard in childhood." A good reminder of the primitive, childlike nature of the most precious things.

43
First Question: What's Really Going On?

I well recall comments from jail inmates as well as unhoused persons when expressing their frustration over glacial change in "the system." More often than not conversations would revolve back to a timely and timeless question: "What's Really Going On?" I would hear personal experiences of the "goings on" and sometimes the "Bigger Picture" would come into focus. In these moments, it was my turn to listen and learn. I could only nod and shake my head until more thinking was stimulated.

In an email exchange on homelessness with a Christian friend, he zeroed in on a particular concern: the incredibly high costs of sheltering people. In my response I agreed, then called attention to the high cost of human suffering, and that it's our responsibility. Referring to an article in our hometown paper, I wrote: "With literally hundreds of churches and various congregations in the region. . .how is it someone like this woman and her son can't find housing?"

The article stated:

"The family is on multiple wait lists for permanent housing, but until a spot opens — which could take more than a year — no one seems to know how to help them. [Her son's] disability makes staying in an emergency shelter difficult and, she recently learned, nearly impossible."

This lady was still searching for real answers: "Where is she supposed to go while they wait for housing? Who qualifies for subsidized motel stays, if not her family? And why is finding help so difficult?"

In my friend's view: "Churches usually don't respond either because they are focused on caring for their own congregation or have already committed to a ministry." He went on to explain that churches, small businesses and other service agencies are "overwhelmed with requests for support." He emphasized there are people without homes everywhere.

I don't dispute that. Of course the human tragedy is all across the nation. We're all overwhelmed. But not as overwhelmed as those experiencing homelessness. My issue, in this case, is the purpose of religious groups. As I wrote:

"You're absolutely right, there are people seeking housing here, there and everywhere. And, sure, there are many organizations (and lots of money, as you point out), and many congregations too, trying to address a rather overwhelming human situation." Then I spoke to a central concern of mine: "I have simply wondered, for a very long time, how religious institutions can, in good conscience, say they follow a poor, homeless, criminalized person, and not put the lion's share of their (tax exempt) money, effort and property into human service. As a former minister, I don't think clergy should have large salaries and large homes anyway. As long as "holy places" and "sanctuaries" are closed and locked most of the time, the least of these will live outside, presumably with the Nazarene," adding:

"(wouldn't it be great to see "Mega-shelters" or "Mega-villages" instead of "Mega-churches"?)." He agreed with me there. In conclusion, I wrote: "By the way, a pastor I used to work with ended services each Sunday with the words: "The worship is over, let the service begin." I liked that. One hour for worship, the rest of the week is serving others." Again, he thought that was good.

I've engaged these kinds of conversations for years both inside and outside ministry and the church. My disappointment with the response of the religious community overall is at least one reason I left ministry, church and faith. Now, as a humanist, I'm as troubled as ever by the "Great Distraction" that is theology, worship, prayer, bible-studying and any beliefs that focus on faith as the primary activity of believers.

In order to have any sense for what is "really going on," we have to pay better attention, listen, learn and listen more. If all we see is an "issue" or "problem," and what concerns us most is the "cost," a clear mirror—or clean window—may reveal what is really going on *with us*—this may be *our issue and problem* that will cost us a little more thought and effort. Uncomfortable to face, perhaps, but much more real.

I don't have the answers or solutions to poverty and its many consequences (I used to suggest sincere people get to know one person or one family at a time, listen, and do what's best). As I say, there are many forms of solutions or means to address poverty, and maybe responses we haven't thought of yet.

What I *do* have is many years of thinking about it, working among those who suffer through, listening to them, learning from them, to learn over and over that until we finally learn *they are us*, our neighbors, a part of our community, no significant solutions will "find a home" in our cities.

44
Is a Creator Playing Hide-and-Seek?

Among the top go-to sources I click to for news and, well honestly, interesting stuff, is BBC.com. During one particular morning of clicking around the site, flicking by fascinating reads like "The Mouse with Super-healing Powers" and "The Forest Tended by an Elusive Giant," an article on particles collided with my attention span. That's a hint at the subject: the Cern collider in Switzerland ("Large hadron collider: A revamp that could revolutionise physics," April, 2022). I wouldn't pretend to grasp even a particle of understanding here, but I did find the comments from physicists explosive.

One Dr. Harper explains: "I've been hunting for the fifth force for as long as I've been a particle physicist." We all have some comprehension (I think) when we're talking about gravity, magnetism and several little nuclear things (my sophistication is showing), but scientists are spending big time and big money to build big machines to find ... the smallest bits of the universe. This would blow my mind, if my mind could even imagine a "small bit" that might possibly hold everything together. As the article describes the exciting challenge: "As well as believing that they may find a new, fifth force of nature, researchers hope to find evidence of an invisible substance that makes up most of the Universe called Dark Matter."

Here's where my brain matter shrinks to a neutron. Then, I'm energized by the electrons of theological questions. The scientific pursuit of knowledge, particularly about particles, building-blocks of our universe, may have something to say about the eternal religious pursuit of the Building-Block Maker.

This thought collides with one troubling fact: As we discover more blocks, we aren't uncovering an Undercover Personality. Unless of course, as I'll mention below, one believes the blocks themselves are a deity.

Do you ever wonder why a Creator of such marvels, mysteries and matter would hide behind a cloak or curtain? Wouldn't you want to stand out in the open and proudly announce: "Hey, look what I made!"?

Instead, like the tiniest bits of the cosmos—like the known and unknown creative forces—any Creative Force remains incognito, beyond cognition.

This leads me to speculate as to the reason such a being would hide:

1) Perhaps, like the parent of a toddler, this Creator is standing back watching as we "learn to walk"—hoping that one day we will toddle back and show gratitude—maybe a type of Deistic image
2) Perhaps, like a professor, this Creator has written everything we need to know on the black blackboard or white whiteboard of the universe and the rest is a test—maybe a more philosophical image
3) Perhaps, like a practical joker, this Creator is having fun, playing with us—a great galactic game of hide-and-seek—maybe a lighter, more insouciant image

As I see it there may be one other option:

4) Perhaps (as some believers, including some believing physicists believe), like a pantheistic potentate, this Creator IS the creation, IS the particle, and every particle—God is Nature and Nature is God kind of image (all images colliding into one)

So where does this leave us? Some people of faith might believe in a blend of these views. They may feel that the Creator is a parent, professor, somewhat playful, as well as an essential part of everything. Others may hold one or more of these images.

Near the conclusion of the BBC article, Dr. Harper

reveals his concerns: "Because the worst thing in the world will be that the new physics is there, and we don't find it." His enthusiasm propels his research forward: "The thing that drives all particle physicists is that we want to discover the unknown and this is why things like the fifth force and dark matter are so exciting because we have no idea what it could be or if it exists and we really want to find this out."

Is this what religion is doing? Is this similar to what faith seeks? Or, could it be said that religious faith actually avoids the whole enterprise since faith is quite often not concerned with exploring new questions and frontiers, of revealing the unknowns? A scientist who is a person of faith might say the more we discover in nature, the more we uncover the creativity of the Creator. No doubt there are scientists who believe the "fifth force" may be divine. But what if it collides with their theology?

The question cycles back: Why stay hidden? Why appear to be playing an eternal game of hide-and-seek with a massively minute mass of matter called Humanity?

I'd like a proton more light on this before I collide with the problem again.

45
Opening Thoughts at the Closing of the Book(s)

Reflecting on reflection, I find myself gazing deeper into the ways and means by which Nature reflects life, me, everything. If you've seen some of my photography or read my poetry you know I can't resist bubbles, streams, rivers, lakes, raindrops, insect eyes. I look up at the sky and down at a puddle; ponder how a pond is an ocean, how a leaf is a tree and a tree is a leaf; a bee mirrors a flower and vice versa—a stinging realization of life's reflections. All images seem to pull me in close to reflect on where I stand not just in relation but in reflection to the world.

"We want to stand upon our own feet and look fair and square at the world—its good facts, its bad facts, its beauties, and its ugliness; see the world as it is and be not afraid of it. . . . A good world needs knowledge, kindliness, and courage … ." (Bertrand Russell, *Why I Am Not a Christian*, 1927)

As I described in chapter 18, an emergency eye appointment opened my eyes to some facts: I'm aging, and, I don't know much! I didn't know that many people my age see "floaters" in their eyes. I'm on the edge of cataracts, and was afraid I was experiencing a "detached retina." Relieved to hear it wasn't serious, over the next few weeks my vision adjusted and I wasn't distracted by the floaters much any longer. Isn't it amazing how the brain can recalibrate and rebalance? I have to ask: Why do I need these recurrent reminders that sight is a precious thing never to lose sight of? Fact is, I don't actually need the reminder since the thought of life's short span has been in clear view for a long time. But I still need to have these moments to think: "Oh, yeah, I remember, I see."

When posting several photos of our local bears I wrote: "A shadow appears at the corner of my eye. I glance out the window. A black shape passes. Immediate action! Grab my *phonera* (phone+camera) and walk quickly to the window, crouching. Around the corner a large shape appears. No time to open the door to get a close up … and might be good I didn't, since the Big Mama Bear was close! As she ambled by, I clicked a few shots. She didn't turn, didn't see me."

I live for these moments. Surprised by nature, feeling so close to nature, yet just beyond my reach and maybe the reach of my vision. As I wrote earlier, what's really going on in the natural environment around me? How deeply am I immersed in it? I mean, seriously, how close can I be to the bear, or other creature, or the forest? I know I'm connected, but there are too many floaters in the way. My peripheral vision is still good, but not quite that good. Some reflections can be blinding, like the flashes I saw when my floaters first appeared.

So I read and keep reading. As long as I can, I'll continue to find new books and read them, to soak in more knowledge about the Great Book we truly live in —some chapters open, others closed, to us, for now. Some don't care if the Great Book burns to a crisp or gets waterlogged and dissolves, ink running into dark and dead rivers. Others have latched onto a page or two and made their home inside, deciding those few words or sentences are all they need. But oh, the book is so much greater and grander.

One Nature indivisible, cohesive, coalescing, coagulating. One Book incandescent, virescent. Try to cut Nature, the Book, into pieces and ignore the storylines, the interlaced roots, and it feels unhealthy, unreal, unnatural, because it is. Try to slice it into one part natural and one part supernatural, or claim it's all about the Author and the book really doesn't amount to more than a pile of paper. We feel the disconnect, dissected by all that is divisible into black holes and bosons, Milky Ways and milky substances—blood, sperm or amniotic fluid—humans and other living things, and on and on into the nearest or farthest reaches.

How do we make the indivisibility visible? Break the borders of our brains, or the imagined limits of them, and see where it takes us. We need to make a pledge to free opinions and the search for truth. As Paine said at the conclusion of *The Age of Reason*: "[I am] certain, that when opinions are free, either in matters of government or religion, truth will finally and powerfully prevail." Along the way to wherever that truth takes us, we find guidance in those great minds who had the vision to see the unseeable Greatness of the Great Book. "Truth can stand by itself," wrote Thomas Jefferson—"Subject opinion to coercion: whom will you make your inquisitors?" (*Notes on the State of Virginia*, 1782).

And so our pledge begins to form. *I pledge allegiance to truth, reason, others, the earth.* Naturalist and philosopher John Burroughs strikes another match to the candle, a blinding spark: "The great mother church may draw her curtains and re-trim her lamps and make believe it is still night in the world, but those outside know better, and those inside are bound to find it out by and by." (*The Light of Day*, 1904). And we are found out, as we see more, and see better.

Good bless the visionaries: the Three Mothers,

Sagan and Equiano, Koheleth and Jesus, Dunbar and Hurston, Seneca and Thoreau, and the seekers present and future, you and me. If we only see floaters we get distracted by things like theology. The hide and seek never stops, but it's we who seek because it's we who are hidden, who hide from ourselves and the Nature that we are.

The afternoon that mama bear and cubs ambled by, I jotted this: "Smiling, I was happy to see my visiting neighbors …And THEN, another cub! Running too quick to catch an image. I welcome the Wild. Daily wild, inside and outside. Never (or rarely, barely) unbearable."

Catch a glimpse, catch an image, catch an idea, catch Life and the too-large-to-catch *Everything* to name it, to call it something, so we call it Nature. Too big to hold in our hands, too massive to manage in our minds. Ah, but it's all we have, and it has us. There's hardly time to rest, or live, or die.

With every book that closes, another opens, because, truth is—it's all Book, some pages intriguingly obscure, others always and forever laid open and inviting.

ABOUT THE AUTHOR

Chris Highland was born and raised in the Pacific Northwest and lived for over 35 years in the San Francisco Bay Area. He was a Protestant minister and Interfaith chaplain for many years before becoming a Humanist celebrant.

With a degree in Religion and Philosophy from an evangelical Christian university (Seattle Pacific) and a Master of Divinity degree from a diverse consortium of seminaries (Graduate Theological Union in Berkeley), he has been active in "presence ministry" and nonprofit work in a private school, a county jail, homeless shelters and affordable housing.

He is the author of many books including essay collections, secular biblical studies, poetry and a novella. He teaches courses on Freethought at the

Reuter Center on the campus of the University of North Carolina, Asheville.

Chris holds membership in the American Humanist Association, Americans United for Separation of Church and State, the Freedom From Religion Foundation and the Religious Naturalist Association.

Since 2016 he has been writing weekly "Highland Views" columns for the Asheville *Citizen-Times* (a USA Today affiliate) addressing major religious and theological questions as well as playful and sensitive issues of faith and secularism.

Chris and his wife Carol, a Presbyterian minister, live on the Blue Ridge Mountains, near Great Smoky Mountains National Park, in Asheville, North Carolina.

His primary website is:

Friendly Freethinker (www.chighland.com)

To contact Chris:

chris.highland@gmail.com

Made in the USA
Coppell, TX
28 October 2022